Riding the Wave

Workbook

Donna B. Pincus • Jill T. Ehrenreich • David A. Spiegel

OXFORD
UNIVERSITY PRESS

2008

OXFORD
UNIVERSITY PRESS

Oxford University Press, Inc., publishes works that further
Oxford University's objective of excellence
in research, scholarship, and education.

Oxford   New York
Auckland   Cape Town   Dar es Salaam   Hong Kong   Karachi
Kuala Lumpur   Madrid   Melbourne   Mexico City   Nairobi
New Delhi   Shanghai   Taipei   Toronto

With offices in
Argentina   Austria   Brazil   Chile   Czech Republic   France   Greece
Guatemala   Hungary   Italy   Japan   Poland   Portugal   Singapore
South Korea   Switzerland   Thailand   Turkey   Ukraine   Vietnam

Published by Oxford University Press, Inc.
198 Madison Avenue, New York, New York 10016

www.oup.com

Oxford is a registered trademark of Oxford University Press

ISBN-978-0-19-533581-1

Chapter 1

Getting Started

You are about to begin a treatment program designed specifically for teens with panic disorder (PD). Over the next 12 weeks, you will meet with your therapist to learn skills that you can use to relieve your feelings of fear and anxiety. Before you begin however, it is important to make sure that this program is right for you.

What Is Panic Disorder?

PD is a common and treatable disorder. More than 3 million Americans will experience PD during their lifetime. PD often begins during adolescence, although it may start during childhood, and it sometimes runs in families. Children and adolescents with PD have unexpected and repeated periods or "waves" of intense fear or discomfort, along with other scary bodily sensations such as a racing heartbeat or feeling short of breath. These periods or waves are called *panic attacks* and they can last anywhere from a few minutes to a few hours. Panic attacks seem to arise without warning.

Symptoms of a panic attack include:

- Heart pounding or rapid heartbeat

- Sweating

- Trembling or shaking

- Shortness of breath or smothering sensations

- Feeling of choking

- Chest pain or discomfort

- Nausea or stomach discomfort

- Feeling dizzy, unsteady, lightheaded, or faint

- Feeling that the surroundings are unreal or of being detached from oneself

- Numbness or tingling sensations

- Chills or hot flushes

- Fear of losing control or going crazy

- Fear of dying

If not recognized and treated, PD and its complications can be overwhelming. It can interfere with your relationships, schoolwork, and everyday activities. It can make you feel anxious most of the time, even when you are not having a panic attack. You may even begin to avoid situations where you fear a panic attack may occur or situations where help may not be available. This pattern of avoiding certain places or situations is called *agoraphobia,* and it is a common complication of PD. Some examples of places and situations that people with agoraphobia might avoid include:

- Driving or riding in a car in an unfamiliar area, on certain roads or highways, over bridges, or through tunnels

- Being in a shopping mall or certain stores

- Being in crowded places or large open spaces

- Traveling in a subway, train, bus, airplane, or boat

- Taking the escalator

- Riding in an elevator or being in a small, windowless room

- Going to a dentist, doctor, hairdresser, or barber

- Waiting in a line at a checkout counter

- Walking, especially in unfamiliar places or away from home

- Being home alone

- Being away from parents or other loved ones

- Going outside a familiar area

- Being out of town

- Eating in a restaurant, especially an expensive one

- Sitting in a theater, auditorium, classroom, or church, especially in the middle of a row

- Being away from your car or an exit

- Going to school

- Spending time with friends in social activities

- Going to a movie

Do You Have Panic Disorder?

To determine whether or not you have PD, two necessary features must be present. First, you must have experienced *at least two panic attacks* that seemed to come from "out of the blue." And second, the attacks must have been so upsetting to you that they *significantly affected your life for at least a month.* These effects include constant concern or worry that you will have more panic attacks and that they will cause you physical or psychological harm.

The following "yes" or "no" questions will help you figure out if you have PD and/or agoraphobia.

Have you had panic attacks? *Y or N*	To determine this, answer the following three questions: 1. Have you experienced discrete episodes of intense fear or discomfort? Discrete means that the episode had a distinct beginning—that is, you were able say that it started at a certain time. Y or N 2. If so, were any of the episodes accompanied by symptoms from at least four of the 13 categories listed on pages 1 and 2? Y or N 3. If so, during the episodes that included at least four types of symptoms, did the symptoms reach a peak within 10 minutes from the time the episode began? How long they lasted is not important, only how long it took to reach their maximum intensity. Y or N If you answered yes to questions 1–3, you have had panic attacks as they are defined in psychiatry. Panic attacks are necessary for a diagnosis of panic disorder (PD) but are not enough. To determine whether you may have PD, answer questions 4–7.
Could you have panic disorder? *Y or N*	4. Have you had at least two panic attacks (that met the criteria in questions 1–3) that did not seen to be triggered by anything—that is, that seemed to come from out of the blue? Y or N 5. Has the possibility that the attacks were due to a medical problem or to a drug or medication you were taking been considered and rejected? PD sufferers often worry that their attacks are due to an unrecognized medical illness, but answer yes to this question if no evidence of a medical or drug cause has been found. Y or N 6. Has the possibility that the attacks were due to a mental condition other than PD (for example, a specific phobia or social anxiety disorder) been considered and rejected? Y or N <div align="right">*(continued)*</div>

	7. Since your first panic attack, has there been at least a month during which you were constantly concerned about having more attacks, or worried about what the attacks might mean or what consequences they might have, or changed your behavior significantly because of the attacks? Y or N
	If you answered yes to questions 4–7, you may have PD. You should consult a qualified professional to confirm that.

Could you have agoraphobia?
 	
Y or N
	To determine this, answer the following questions:
	
	8. Do you feel anxious about being in places or situations that would be difficult or embarrassing to leave, or where help may not be available if you had a panic attack or panic-like sensations? Y or N
	
	9. If so, do you:
	
	    a. Avoid any of those situations? Y or N
	
	    b. When you are in any of those situations, feel very distressed or anxious about having a panic attack or panic-like sensations? Y or N
	
	    c. Need to have someone along with you to go into those situations? Y or N
	
	10. If so, has the possibility that the anxiety is due to a mental condition other than agoraphobia (for example, a specific phobia or social anxiety disorder) been considered and rejected? Y or N
	
	If you answered yes to questions 8 and 10 and to any of questions 9a–9c, you may have agoraphobia. You should consult a qualified professional to confirm that.

PD and agoraphobia symptoms tend to vary over time. Whether or not you need treatment for them depends upon how upsetting the symptoms are to you (and your family) and whether they prevent you from doing things that you would like to do or that the majority of teenagers your age like to do. Several questionnaires can be used to rate the degree of distress and interference your symptoms are causing. By completing these questionnaires at various times during treatment, it is possible to evaluate how much you have improved. One questionnaire of this kind is the Panic Disorder Severity Scale. People who have been diagnosed with PD typically have total scores of 8 or higher on this scale. But people who score less than that may still benefit from treatment.

Panic Disorder Severity Scale

Date: _____

Instructions: Several of the following questions refer to panic attacks and limited symptom attacks. For this questionnaire, a *panic attack* is defined as a *sudden rush* of fear or discomfort accompanied by *at least four of the symptoms listed below.* To qualify as a sudden rush, the symptoms must *peak within 10 minutes.* Episodes like panic attacks, but having fewer than four of the listed symptoms, are called *limited-symptom attacks.* Here are the symptoms to count:

- Rapid or pounding heartbeat

- Sweating

- Trembling or shaking

- Breathlessness

- Feeling of choking

- Chest pain or discomfort

- Nausea

- Dizziness or faintness

- Feelings of unreality

- Numbness or tingling

- Chills or hot flushes

- Fear of losing control or going crazy

- Fear of dying

For each of the following questions, circle the number of the answer that best describes your experience during the *past week*:

1. How many panic and limited-symptom attacks did you have during the past week?

   0—No panic or limited-symptom episodes

   1—Mild: No full panic attacks and no more than one limited-symptom attack/day

   2—Moderate: One or two full panic attacks and/or multiple limited-symptom attacks/day

   3—Severe: More than two full attacks but not more than one per day on average

   4—Extreme: Full panic attacks occurred more than once a day, more days than not

2. If you had any panic attacks during the past week, how distressing (uncomfortable, frightening) were they *while they were happening*? (If you had more than one, give an average rating. If you didn't have any panic attacks but did have limited-symptom attacks, answer for the limited-symptom attacks.)

   0—Not at all distressing, or no panic or limited-symptom attacks during the past week

   1—Mildly distressing (not too intense)

   2—Moderately distressing (intense, but still manageable)

   3—Severely distressing (very intense)

   4—Extremely distressing (extreme distress during all attacks)

3. During the past week, how much have you worried or felt anxious *about when your next panic attack would occur, or about fears related to the attacks* (for example, that they could mean you have physical or mental health problems or could cause you social embarrassment)?

   0—Not at all

   1—Occasionally or only mildly

   2—Frequently or moderately

   3—Very often or to a very disturbing degree

   4—Nearly constantly and to a disabling extent

4. During the past week, were there any *places or situations* (e.g., public transportation, movie theaters, crowds, bridges, tunnels, shopping malls, being alone) you avoided, or felt afraid of (uncomfortable in, wanted to avoid or leave), *because of fear of having a panic attack?* Are there any other situations that you would have avoided or been afraid of if they had come up during the week, for the same reason? If yes to either question, please rate your level of fear and avoidance this past week.

0—None: No fear or avoidance

1—Mild: Occasional fear and/or avoidance, but I could usually confront or endure the situation. There was little or no modification of my lifestyle due to this.

2—Moderate: Noticeable fear and/or avoidance, but still manageable. I avoided some situations but I could confront them with a companion. There was some modification of my lifestyle because of this, but my overall functioning was not impaired.

3—Severe: Extensive avoidance. Substantial modification of my lifestyle was required to accommodate the avoidance, making it difficult to manage usual activities.

4—Extreme: Pervasive disabling fear and/or avoidance. Extensive modification in my lifestyle was required, such that important tasks were not performed.

5. During the past week, were there any *activities* (e.g., physical exertion, taking a hot shower or bath, drinking coffee, watching an exciting or scary movie) that you avoided, or felt afraid of (uncomfortable doing, wanted to avoid or stop), *because they caused physical sensations like those you feel during panic attacks or that you were afraid might trigger a panic attack?* Are there any other activities that you would have avoided or been afraid of if they had come up during the week, for that reason? If yes to either question, please rate your level of fear and avoidance of those activities this past week.

0—No fear or avoidance of situations or activities because of distressing physical sensations

1—Mild: Occasional fear and/or avoidance, but usually I could confront or endure with little distress activities that cause physical sensations. There was little modification of my lifestyle due to this.

2—Moderate: Noticeable avoidance, but still manageable. There was definite, but limited, modification of my lifestyle, such that my overall functioning was not impaired.

3—Severe: Extensive avoidance. There was substantial modification of my lifestyle or interference in my functioning.

4—Extreme: Pervasive and disabling avoidance. There was extensive modification in my lifestyle due to this, such that important tasks or activities were not performed.

6. During the past week, how much did the above symptoms altogether (panic and limited-symptom attacks, worry about attacks, and fear of situations and activities because of attacks) interfere with your *ability to work, go to school, or carry out your responsibilities at home*? (If your work or home responsibilities were less than usual this past week, answer how you think you would have done if the responsibilities had been usual.)

0—No interference with work or home responsibilities

1—Slight interference with work or home responsibilities, but I could do nearly everything I could do if I didn't have these problems

2—Significant interference with work or home responsibilities, but I still could manage to do the things I needed to do

3—Substantial impairment in work or home responsibilities; there were many important things I couldn't do because of these problems

4—Extreme, incapacitating impairment, such that I was essentially unable to manage any work or home responsibilities

7. During the past week, how much did panic and limited-symptom attacks, worry about attacks, and fear of situations and activities because of attacks, interfere with your *social life*? (If you didn't have many opportunities to socialize this past week, answer how you think you would have done if you did have opportunities.)

0—No interference

1—Slight interference with social activities, but I could do nearly everything I could do if I didn't have these problems

2—Significant interference with social activities, but I could manage to do most things if I made the effort

3—Substantial impairment in social activities; there are many social things I couldn't do because of these problems

4—Extreme, incapacitating impairment, such that there was hardly anything social I could do

Your Score (add the seven numbers you circled) _____

Although these questionnaires will help determine whether or not you have PD, it is very important to confirm your diagnosis with a qualified mental health professional. Be sure to bring these completed forms to your first meeting with your therapist. He will review them with you and start you on the treatment program.

Introduction to Program

You are about to begin a treatment program that will teach you the skills you need to overcome your anxiety and fear. You will work with your therapist to identify the factors that cause and maintain your anxiety and learn how to eliminate them from your life. During this program, you will be asked to participate in exercises called "exposures" that will help you to face your anxiety and the scary feelings that go along with it. These exposures may make you feel uncomfortable but, as time goes on and you practice the exercises more and more, your anxiety will decrease greatly. You will learn to "ride the waves" of frightening sensations caused by your panic. Your therapist will give you more detailed information about the treatment during your first session.

Using This Workbook

This workbook contains all the information you will need throughout treatment. It includes summaries of topics you will discuss in sessions with your therapist, as well as homework assignments and the forms you need to complete them. Each chapter of the workbook corresponds to a particular therapy session. After each session with your therapist, you should read the corresponding workbook chapter and complete the quiz at the end. Chapter quizzes are meant to test your knowledge and understanding of the information presented. You will not be graded on them. Quiz answers can be found in the appendix at the back of the workbook. Your therapist will review the answers with you in session and answer any questions you may have.

As mentioned, each chapter of the workbook contains homework assignments for you to do on your own time, outside of the sessions with your therapist. Like the quizzes, you will not be graded on the homework. It is very important to do your best to complete the assignments, however. Practicing the skills you learn on a regular basis is key to your success.

Before your first session, review this chapter and write down any questions you have about the material presented in the space provided so you can discuss them with your therapist. Be sure to bring your workbook to every session.

_____

_____

_____

_____

_____

_____

_____

_____

_____

_____

_____

_____

_____

_____

_____

_____

_____

Session 1
Introduction

Chapter 2

Goals

- To learn about your anxiety and panic

- To learn about this program and set personal goals for treatment

- To begin monitoring your panic attacks

The Pattern of Your Panic

In your first meeting with your therapist, you will review the pretreatment assessment measures you completed in Chapter 1 and talk about your anxiety and panic and the things that cause it.

The causes of your panic are called *triggers* and they can be *internal* or *external*. Internal triggers are things like negative thoughts and physical sensations. External triggers are particular situations that make you feel anxious, like having to give an oral presentation in class.

At first, you may not recognize that there are triggers for your panic. You may think that your panic occurs "out of the blue." To help you identify the triggers for your panic, ask yourself the following questions:

- What usually happens right before a panic attack?

- What is the first thing you feel in your body?

■ What is the first thing you think in your head?

■ What do you imagine might happen when you feel panicky?

You may find it hard to answer these questions because, typically, when you feel anxious or afraid, your attention is focused on the source of danger and the ways you can protect yourself. You aren't necessarily paying attention to the changes that are taking place in your head and in your body. However, it is important to become an "objective observer," because examining your reactions to anxiety and fear in detail can tell you a lot about them. More importantly, self-observation will help you figure out ways to reduce your anxiety and help you be less afraid of panic attacks.

The Nature of Anxiety

Fear and anxiety are natural, necessary, and harmless emotions. They are experienced by everyone and part of the experience of being human. In fact, anxiety can even be helpful. Would you feel scared if a car was driving straight at you? Of course you would! In this case, anxiety and fear about being hit by a car would help you get out of the way. This is called the *fight-or-flight response*. It helps you avoid danger by recognizing an immediate threat and making your body take quick action; either running away or defending yourself. The fight-or-flight response prepares your body to either confront the threat and deal with it, or get as far away from the threat as quickly as possible.

Some people experience the fight-or-flight response when there is no danger present. In these cases, anxiety becomes unhelpful. Anxiety in the absence of danger or threat can make you feel uncomfortable, especially if it occurs too frequently or is really intense.

It is important to understand that fear and anxiety are reactions. From now on, we want you to think of anxiety as something you feel in response to physical feelings in your body, the thoughts that you have, or the situations you are in. If you identify these causes or triggers, you can start to learn how to react to them in a way that will help reduce your anxiety and panic over time. We do not want to take away *all* of your anxiety and fear. Just like the example we gave of getting out of the way of a speeding car, anxiety and fear can help you in genuinely dangerous situations. We only want to reduce the anxiety that does not help you and that you do not need.

The Parts of Anxiety

Anxiety is made up of three parts that work together to cause your fear and panic. They are: feelings, thoughts, and behaviors.

What You Feel

The physical component of fear and anxiety are the sensations you feel in your body during panic. Examples of these feelings include a fast heartbeat, dizziness, feeling unreal, and sweating. These feelings act like an emergency alarm. When you experience these sensations, your body is telling you that you are in danger. When your body gives you a "false alarm," a panic attack happens even though no real threat or danger is present.

The types and strength of the bodily sensations you feel depend upon which system is turned on (anxiety or fear), how strongly, and for how long. With mild or moderate levels of anxiety, common sensations include things like feeling keyed up or on edge, a queasy stomach, irritability, muscle tightness or jitters, and jumpiness. If the anxiety continues over a longer period of time, you can experience muscle aches, headaches, and tiredness. Fear reactions (including panic attacks) can cause sensations of heart racing or pounding, sweating, trembling or shaking, difficulty breathing or swallowing, chest pain, nausea, diarrhea, dizziness or faintness, chills or hot flushes, numbness or tingling sensations, and feelings of unreality. These sensations can be scary, especially when they seem to come from out of the blue, for no apparent reason.

What You Think

The cognitive component of anxiety is the thoughts and images you experience during panic. When you are in a situation that is really dangerous, you may not notice that your heart is racing or that you feel dizzy. If you did notice these feelings, you would consider them normal. After all, almost everyone's heart races when they are scared. However, when your body gives you a false alarm, and there is nothing to be afraid of, the only place to direct your attention is inward. You may start thinking that you are losing control or even that you are dying. You may also feel embarrassed because you are panicking even though there is nothing to be afraid of. Thoughts like these are called "panic thoughts," and they will increase your anxiety because they undermine your ability to handle the situation. As you continue to think negatively, your self-confidence decreases and you become even more panicked.

What You Do

The behavioral component of anxiety is the behaviors that you do because of anxiety and fear. Some are unintentional, meaning that you do them automatically without planning to. Examples of automatic behaviors are startle reactions, facial expressions, gasping or holding your breath, breathing faster, clenching your teeth, pacing, fidgeting, and nervous mannerisms like stroking your hair or chin, clearing your throat, smoothing your clothes, or swinging your foot.

Some behaviors are done on purpose. Examples of these types of behaviors include the things you do to reduce uncomfortable feelings in your body (slowing your breathing, splashing water on your face); assure yourself that you are okay (checking your pulse, swallowing); keep from thinking scary thoughts (distracting yourself); make yourself feel safer (carrying a cell phone or lucky charm, looking for the nearest exit).

One of the most interfering behaviors you can do is avoid or escape from situations or activities that scare you. Avoidance and escape are often common and usually obvious behaviors, although they can take subtle forms. Escape behaviors are the most obvious of these actions, such as abruptly leaving a situation or place where a panic attack may occur, like a restaurant or shopping mall. People with panic disorder often do that when they feel a panic attack coming on. Avoidance most often occurs when a person simply chooses to not enter the situation in the first place. For example, say it is the night before you have to give an oral presentation in class. You are afraid to do it, so you pretend to be sick to get out of going to school the next day. Avoiding or escaping certain situations because of anxiety isn't very helpful. In fact, it can even make your anxiety worse over time. If you avoid or escape from all the things that make you anxious, you never get a chance to practice getting used to them.

How the Parts of Anxiety Work Together

The three parts of anxiety may affect each other in a way that makes your panic and anxiety worse as time goes on. Your brain is like a watchdog that has been trained to be on the lookout for danger. When the watchdog notices anything that seems to signal danger—just like a real dog would, it sends a message to its owner (in this case, your body, which has been trained to listen carefully to the watchdog). So, when you go into a situation where you had a panic attack, the watchdog perks up and says, "Something scary happened here before, I better be on the lookout to make sure nothing dangerous is around."

Your body listens to the watchdog say that something dangerous could happen and responds by starting to prepare for this possibility by making your heart beat a little faster and speeding up your breathing, among other things. When the watchdog, who is looking very carefully for anything that might signal danger, notices that your heart is beating faster, he interprets this as a signal that something scary might happen. He sends a message to your body which says "Oh no! The scary feelings are starting to happen again."

Your body then becomes more alarmed when it hears the watchdog say that something scary might happen, so it gets even more prepared by making your heart beat faster and creating some adrenaline. In this way, your mind and body continue to play off each other in a sort of vicious cycle that leads to a panic attack. When these feelings continue, you may respond by having the urge to avoid or escape ("I need to get out of here!"). However, as we discussed earlier, these responses usually increase anxiety in the long-term because they prevent you from practicing, getting used to, and learning to handle the situation.

The picture shown in Figure 2.1 illustrates how the three parts of anxiety work together to form a cycle.

My Cycle of Panic and Anxiety

Now that you understand the three parts of anxiety and the way they interact with one another, try to apply this new knowledge to your own anxiety and panic. Describe one of your recent panic attacks, and fill out the form on page 19. You will complete this form throughout the remainder of treatment each time you experience a panic attack. An additional blank copy can

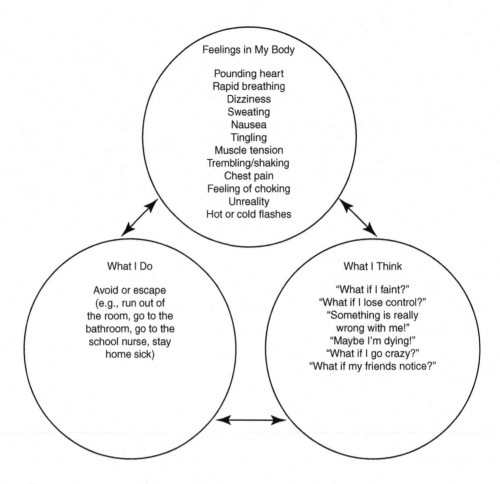

Figure 2.1 The Cycle of Panic and Anxiety

My Cycle of Panic and Anxiety

Name _____

Date _____ Time _____ Duration _____ (mins)

With: Family member _____ Friend _____ Stranger _____ Alone _____

Stressful situation: Yes/No   If yes, specify _____   Expected: Yes/No

Maximum Anxiety (Circle the number that applies)

0 ·············· 1 ·············· 2 ·············· 3 ·············· 4 ·············· 5 ·············· 6 ·············· 7 ·············· 8

None   Moderate   Extreme

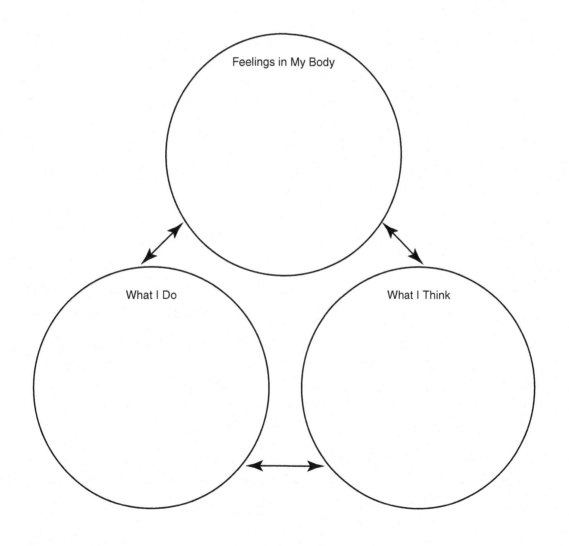

be found at the end of the chapter and every chapter that follows. Extra copies are available in an appendix at the back of this workbook. If you find that you need more than what we have provided, please feel free to make photocopies.

Overview of the Program

Your first panic attack probably happened during a time when you felt stressed. Now, you have panic attacks because you are afraid of feeling the physical sensations of anxiety (racing heart, breathlessness, sweating, etc.). You are also afraid of how these feelings affect your thoughts and behaviors. This is what keeps your anxiety going. Refer back to your personalized cycle of panic and anxiety. This treatment will help you identify the factors that maintain your panic and teach you strategies for handling the three parts of anxiety.

Handling Your Thoughts

You will learn to identify and challenge the assumptions and inaccurate thoughts you have that increase your anxiety and cause panic attacks. To master this technique, you will need to "become a detective" and treat your thoughts like guesses, not facts. You will learn to examine the evidence that supports your thoughts and evaluate the likelihood that the bad things you think are going to happen actually will.

Handling Your Feelings

You will participate in exercises that help you become less afraid of the physical feelings caused by panic. These exercises will recreate the bodily sensations caused by anxiety. Although this may be scary at first, the more you expose yourself to the feelings, the more you'll be able to handle them.

Handling Your Actions

You will learn to stop avoiding and escaping and gradually face certain situations that make you anxious. By facing situations that cause panic attacks, you will learn that the things you are afraid of (like fainting or going crazy) do not happen. By staying in the situation long enough, you will have a chance for your feelings of panic to come down on their own. Facing situations repeatedly will decrease your fear and make you more confident in your ability to handle your anxiety and panic.

The overall goal of treatment is to "break the cycle" of panic by dealing with each component of anxiety individually.

Practicing Skills and Keeping Track of Your Anxiety

Practice

Treatment involves learning skills. Like any skill (such as learning to ride a bicycle), these skills need to be practiced on a regular basis. The more you practice on your own, the more likely you are to benefit from this program.

Keeping Track

A big part of this program is keeping track of your anxiety and panic. Monitoring your attacks and the where and when (the context) in which they happen will help you become an expert at describing and understanding your anxiety.

In addition to completing the My Cycle of Panic and Anxiety form each time you experience a panic attack, you will use the Weekly Record to record your daily levels of anxiety, depression, and pleasantness. Anxiety and depression frequently go hand-in-hand. Keeping track of both can help you see the relationship between the two and how improving your anxiety can also improve your depression. "Pleasantness" is a general sense of feeling good. It is helpful to record how good you feel each day because it will show you that, although you are having trouble with anxiety, you are still able to get enjoyment out of life.

A blank copy of the Weekly Record can be found at the end of the chapter and every chapter that follows. Additional copies are available in an appendix at the back of this workbook. If you find that you need extras, please feel free to make photocopies.

Your Goals for Treatment

Now that you have reviewed the basic purpose of treatment and the types of feelings you will be working on, you and your therapist will work together to set the expectations and goals you have for treatment. Complete the My Goals form that follows and review it with your therapist.

My Goals

Use the space provided to write down goals you would like to achieve. Pick things you really want to change and explain some of the reasons why you think they are important to you. Also include specific steps you can take to achieve these goals. Use the examples to help you as you fill out each section.

My Goals – These are the goals I want to achieve:

Example – *To enjoy skateboarding and hanging out with my friends again*

1. _____

2. _____

3. _____

4. _____

My Reasons – These are my reasons for wanting to accomplish these goals:

Example – *To feel happy like I used to and enjoy senior year with my friends*

1. _____

2. _____

3. _____

4. _____

The Steps – These are the steps I can take to meet my goals:

Example – *Come to therapy and skateboard with my friends even if I don't want to at first*

1. _____

2. _____

3. _____

4. _____

The Signs – I will know that I am achieving my goals if:

Example – *I hang out with my friends more and feel excited about skateboarding again*

1. _____

2. _____

3. _____

_____

Weighing Your Options

It is important that you understand that treatment may not always be easy. You will be asked to try new things to see if these new actions or ways of dealing with your feelings are more helpful. You may also gain some other very positive things from treatment. For homework, you will be asked to complete the Weighing My Options form provided here. This form will help you determine the costs and benefits of participating in this program.

Weighing My Options

When we think about making a change, it's sometimes hard to see all sides. We may ignore things we don't want to do or feel are too hard to do. Use the following form to evaluate your choices and help you think through all the pros and cons. Pick a behavior that you might consider changing and evaluate the costs and benefits of staying the same and the costs and benefits of changing. Use Mike's example about trying to call his mom less frequently to help you fill out the form for yourself.

Benefits of NO change – Reasons it's good for things to stay the same:

Mike – *I have a better chance of knowing my mom is safe if I call her all the time*

1. _____

2. _____

3. _____

4. _____

Costs of NO change – Reasons it's hard for things to stay the same:

Mike – *I'll keep feeling sick at basketball whenever my mom is late*

1. _____

2. _____

3. _____

4. _____

Benefits of Change – Reasons it would be good for things to change:

Mike – *I can do more with my friends and I won't bother my mom as much*

1. _____

2. _____

3. _____

4. _____

Costs of Change – Reasons it would be hard for things to change:

Mike – *At first I might worry more about my mom if I don't know for sure she is OK*

1. _____

2. _____

3. _____

Homework

- Review this chapter and complete the quiz

- Record the number of panic attacks and your daily levels of anxiety, depression, and pleasantness over the course of the next week using the Weekly Record found at the end of this chapter

- Use the My Cycle of Panic and Anxiety form to record the details of each individual panic attack you experience

- Review the My Goals form

- Complete the Weighing My Options form

Quiz

1. What are triggers? Give examples of internal and external triggers.

_____

_____

_____

_____

2. What does the "fight-or-flight response" prepare your body to do?

_____

_____

_____

_____

3. What are the three parts of anxiety? Give examples of each.

_____

_____

_____

_____

_____

Weekly Record

Name: _____   Date: _____

Each evening, please make the following ratings, using the scale below:

1. Your AVERAGE level of anxiety of that day.
2. Your MAXIMUM level of anxiety experienced at any one point in the day.
3. Your AVERAGE level of depression that day.
4. Your MAXIMUM level of depression experienced at any one point in the day.
5. Your AVERAGE level of pleasantness that day.
6. Your MAXIMUM level of pleasantness experienced that day.
7. Number of panic attacks experienced, if any.

Level of Anxiety/Depression/Pleasantness

0	1	2	3	4	5	6	7	8
None		Slight		Moderate		A lot		As much as I can imagine

Date	Average Anxiety	Maximum Anxiety	Average Depression	Maximum Depression	Average Pleasantness	Maximum Pleasantness	Panic Attacks

My Cycle of Panic and Anxiety

Name _____

Date _____ Time _____ Duration _____ (mins)

With: Family member _____ Friend _____ Stranger _____ Alone _____

Stressful situation: Yes/No   If yes, specify _____   Expected: Yes/No

Maximum Anxiety (Circle the number that applies)

0 ·········· 1 ·········· 2 ·········· 3 ·········· 4 ·········· 5 ·········· 6 ·········· 7 ·········· 8

None   Moderate   Extreme

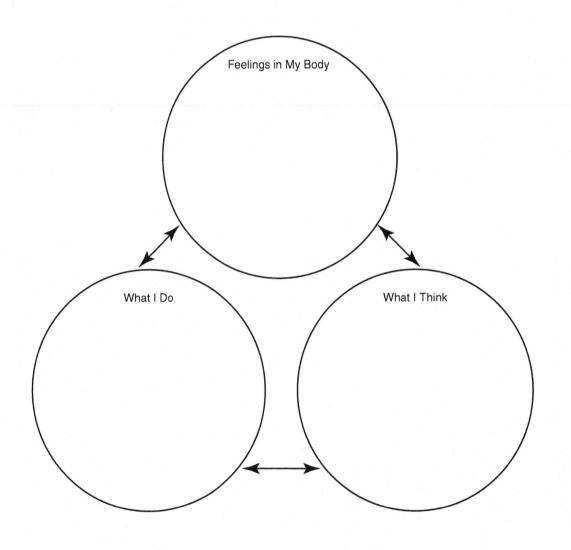

Chapter

3

Session 2
Anxious
Feelings

Goals

■ To learn more about what you feel when you are anxious

■ To learn about hyperventilation and how it can impact your anxiety

Physical Component of Anxiety

As discussed in Chapter 2, the physical sensations of panic are reactions in your body that occur when you are faced with danger. These sensations signal the activation of the *fight-or-flight response* (see Chapter 2 for more detail) and affect many systems of the body.

Heart

When you are faced with danger, your heart begins to pump faster and harder to get more blood and oxygen to parts of the body that will be used to fight or flee (run away). This can be felt as your heart beating very fast. Blood is also directed toward large muscle groups needed for running (such as thighs) or fighting (biceps). This means that blood is redirected away from the skin and smaller muscles, which can make your hands feel cold.

Breathing

To get more oxygen to the parts of your body that will be used to fight off danger or escape from it, you need to breathe faster and deeper than normal. You may feel like you are breathing heavy, you may experience pains and tightness in your chest and, in some instances, you may feel breathless. In addition, since blood is being redirected toward large muscle groups, areas that are getting less blood are also getting less oxygen, although not enough to be dangerous. This can be felt as tingling or numbness in your fingers, dizziness, and lightheadedness.

Sweating

Activation of the fight-or-flight system is hard work, so your body begins to sweat to cool down. Another benefit to sweating is that it makes skin more slippery and harder for a predator or attacker to grab on to.

Miscellaneous

The pupils of your eyes dilate to let in more light, which can result in blurred vision or spots in front of your eyes. Salivation decreases, which results in a dry mouth. Muscles tense to prepare for fight-or-flight, which can create feelings of tension and muscle aches, as well as trembling.

Summary

The sensations of panic happen automatically in response to danger or threat and serve to protect you by activating the fight-or-flight response. The purpose of these sensations is to physically prepare your body for action (such as fighting or fleeing). In the times of our distant ancestors, who were mostly hunters and gatherers, it was very important that an automatic response took over that caused immediate action when danger was present. For example, when a vicious lion appeared, our ancestors had to immediately attack or run in order not to be killed. Even today, this kind of automatic response is necessary—for example, when a car is speeding toward you.

Hyperventilation

Hyperventilation is when you breathe faster and deeper than is necessary. Many people hyperventilate during anxiety, and this can produce some of the symptoms of panic and anxiety.

The most important thing to understand about hyperventilation is that, although it can *feel* as if you don't have enough oxygen, the *opposite* is true. With hyperventilation, your body has *too much* oxygen. To use this oxygen, your body needs a certain amount of carbon dioxide. When you hyperventilate, you do not give your body long enough to retain carbon dioxide, and so your body cannot use the oxygen you have. This causes you to feel as if you are short of air, when actually you have too much.

In today's session, your therapist will conduct a hyperventilation exercise with you. The purpose of the exercise is to demonstrate that the simple act of hyperventilating or over-breathing can cause symptoms similar to those you experience during panic. It is important to remember that hyperventilation can occur in other ways that are not as dramatic or obvious as observed during the exercise. For example, rapid, shallow breathing, frequent sighing, or frequent yawning results in low carbon dioxide levels in the body. People can hyperventilate without even realizing it.

Hyperventilation is not dangerous. As soon as you stop hyperventilating, your body returns to its normal state, and panic symptoms disappear.

Homework

- Review this chapter and complete the quiz

- Continue recording the number of panic attacks and your daily levels of anxiety, depression, and pleasantness over the course of the next week using the Weekly Record found at the end of this chapter

- Use the My Cycle of Panic and Anxiety form to record the details of each individual panic attack you experience

Quiz

1. What are some of the physical sensations of the fight-or-flight response?

_____

_____

_____

_____

2. What is hyperventilation?

_____

_____

_____

_____

3. What was the purpose of the hyperventilation exercise?

_____

_____

_____

_____

Weekly Record

Name: _____   Date: _____

Each evening, please make the following ratings, using the scale below:

1. Your AVERAGE level of anxiety of that day.
2. Your MAXIMUM level of anxiety experienced at any one point in the day.
3. Your AVERAGE level of depression that day.
4. Your MAXIMUM level of depression experienced at any one point in the day.
5. Your AVERAGE level of pleasantness that day.
6. Your MAXIMUM level of pleasantness experienced that day.
7. Number of panic attacks experienced, if any.

Level of Anxiety/Depression/Pleasantness

0	1	2	3	4	5	6	7	8
None		Slight		Moderate		A lot		As much as I can imagine

Date	Average Anxiety	Maximum Anxiety	Average Depression	Maximum Depression	Average Pleasantness	Maximum Pleasantness	Panic Attacks

My Cycle of Panic and Anxiety

Name _____

Date _____ Time _____ Duration _____ (mins)

With: Family member _____ Friend _____ Stranger _____ Alone _____

Stressful situation: Yes/No   If yes, specify _____   Expected: Yes/No

Maximum Anxiety (Circle the number that applies)

o ·········· I ·········· 2 ·········· 3 ·········· 4 ·········· 5 ·········· 6 ·········· 7 ·········· 8

None   Moderate   Extreme

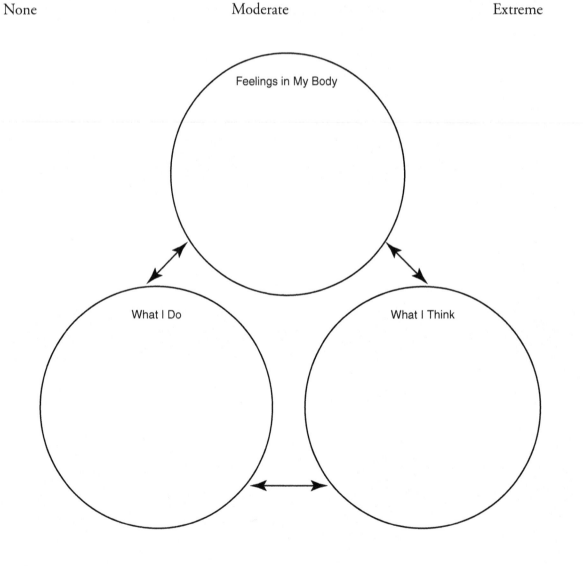

Session 3
Anxious Thoughts

Chapter 4

Goals

- To learn more about what you think when you are anxious

- To learn about errors in thinking and how to identify your anxious thoughts

- To begin monitoring your thoughts every time you experience a panic attack

Cognitive Component of Anxiety

As briefly discussed in Chapter 1, anxiety and panic can affect your thoughts. When you sense that you are in danger, you scan your surroundings and focus your attention on the source of the potential threat. When no real danger or threat can be found, however, the search for danger is turned inward. You become preoccupied with thoughts about how your anxiety is affecting you. You may feel like you are dying or that you are losing control. You may think, "If nothing *out there* is making me feel anxious, there must be something wrong *inside* me." As you learned in Session 1, these thoughts are called *panic thoughts*, and they can interfere with your concentration and memory.

Constantly thinking about and anticipating future panic attacks makes you feel tense and like you are always on "high alert." This apprehension keeps the panic cycle continuing. Think of how you might feel if swimming at a beach where a shark had recently been seen. You would be constantly on the lookout for any signs of possible danger. For example, you may think that minnows moving through the water or seaweed touching your legs were actually a shark, and this would make you feel even more anxious. On the other hand, if you were at a beach where no sharks had ever been seen, you would probably pay very little attention to the minnows or the seaweed, and you would feel much more relaxed. The shark is like the fear of a panic attack, which causes you to be constantly on the lookout for signs of danger.

Or, think how it feels to be home alone, particularly after watching a scary movie. You might interpret small sounds (such as a bird or squirrel on the roof, or creaking sounds from the house) in a scary way ("Someone's coming to get me!"). In other situations (such as during the day, when others are around, after watching a funny movie), you probably wouldn't even notice these sounds.

Common Anxious Thoughts

Typically, people with panic disorder (PD) have two types of thoughts. The first type of thoughts are called "overestimating" thoughts. The second type of thoughts are the thoughts you have when you "think the worst" is going to happen. These scary thoughts are at the core of your anxiety.

Overestimating

When you overestimate, you are expecting that an unlikely event is going to happen. For example, a lot of people play the lottery because they overestimate their chances of winning. Because they think their odds of winning are good, they go out of their way to buy lottery tickets. Sometimes they even travel far distances or stand in long lines, particularly if the jackpot is big. They may also plan what they'll do with the money "when they win." They get very excited thinking about winning, and then they are very disappointed when they don't.

In the same way, people with anxiety often overestimate the chances that something bad is going to happen. For example, say you have a school dance coming up. You may think to yourself, "I am definitely going to feel sick and will panic at the school dance on Friday night, and I will probably throw up." This is an example of "overestimating," because it is also very possible that you might go to the school dance and not feel sick or panic at all. In fact, there is a good chance that you will actually have fun! Also, if you stopped to think to yourself, "Have I gone to school dances before and not felt sick or panicked?" The answer is probably yes. The likelihood that you will get sick and panic at the dance is very small, even though you are worried that it may happen.

To go back to the example of people who play the lottery: Even though people lose the lottery, they keep on playing thinking that one day they will hit the jackpot. Likewise, even though nothing bad happened when you panicked the last time, you are still afraid of the next panic attack. You might think the only reason you avoided terrible consequences last time was because you had someone there to help you, or you were able to leave the situation. Perhaps you think you have just been lucky, and maybe next time your luck will run out. Or, you have felt anxious about the situation so many times that you automatically have scary thoughts about the situation.

Identifying Your Overestimating Thoughts

Work with your therapist to identify at least two times when you overestimated the chances that you would panic, and write down the thoughts you had in the space provided.

1. _____

2. _____

Try to view anxiety as a buoy on the ocean. When the seas are rough, the buoy gets tossed around. When the seas are calm, the buoy simply floats. The way you think about an event or situation can affect your anxiety or the movement of the buoy. For example, if you interpret your fast heartbeat to mean that you are about to have a heart attack, you will begin to panic, which will only make your heart beat faster (moving the buoy into rough seas). If you interpret your fast heartbeat to mean that you are just nervous or excited, you will begin to relax and your heart rate will slow down (moving the buoy into calm waters).

Thinking the Worst

Another common thought (cognitive error) for people with PD is thinking that the worst thing imaginable is going to happen. This is also called *catastrophic thinking*. Some examples of these types of thoughts are:

- If I faint, I may never regain consciousness.

- If other people noticed that I was having a panic attack, I could never face them again.

- If I have a panic attack at the dance on Friday night, it will be the worst thing in the world.

- If I have a panic attack, I may die.

- If I panic and then throw up, I'll lose all my friends and will wind up being lonely because people will think I am strange.

Identifying Your Catastrophic Thoughts

Work with your therapist to identify at least two of your catastrophic thoughts related to panic and write them in the space provided.

I. _____

2. _____

These kinds of thoughts can cause your anxiety and even make it worse. For example, sometimes when people have catastrophic thoughts, these thoughts can start the whole cycle of anxiety. If you think to yourself, "I will likely panic when I go to the dance on Friday night," then this thought is going to cause panic-like physical reactions in your body. As you walk into the dance, your heart may start to beat faster, your stomach might feel uneasy, and you might feel jittery. All of these physical feelings are getting stirred up to protect you, because you are thinking a thought that is scaring you. This is an example of how thoughts can actually start panic sensations in your body.

Monitoring Your Thoughts

The first step in changing thoughts is learning to identify them, since this can be difficult. It is often hard at first to become more conscious of the thoughts you are having. However, it is very important to start to try to be aware of the thoughts going through your mind that could potentially trigger the cycle of anxiety and panic.

For example, while walking into the dance, you might be more aware of the fact that your heart is racing than what thought you are thinking. If this happens, stop for a second and ask yourself, "What is making my heart race? What am I thinking to myself?" Becoming more aware of what you are thinking is a skill and, with practice, you will become very good at it.

Use the Thought Record provided at the end of the chapter to record your thoughts and beliefs caused by panic. Write down the situation that is causing you to have anxious thoughts, and identify your thoughts using the categories just discussed. Identify the "thinking trap" that you have fallen into. Are you "overestimating" or "thinking the worst?" Do this for each panic and anxiety episode you experience over the course of the next week.

Homework

- Review this chapter and complete the quiz

- Continue recording the number of panic attacks and your daily levels of anxiety, depression, and pleasantness over the course of the next week using the Weekly Record found at the end of this chapter

- Use the My Cycle of Panic and Anxiety form to record the details of each individual panic attack you experience

- Use the Thought Record to record and identify your anxious thoughts for each panic and anxiety episode you experience over the next week

Quiz

1. What are panic thoughts?

_____

_____

_____

_____

2. What are the two types of anxious thoughts that people with PD commonly have?

_____

_____

3. What is overestimating?

_____

_____

_____

_____

4. What is catastrophic thinking?

_____

_____

_____

_____

Thought Record

Situation	Anxious Thought(s)	Identify "Thinking Trap" (Overestimating, Thinking the Worst)

Weekly Record

Name: _____ Date: _____

Each evening, please make the following ratings, using the scale below:

1. Your AVERAGE level of anxiety of that day.
2. Your MAXIMUM level of anxiety experienced at any one point in the day.
3. Your AVERAGE level of depression that day.
4. Your MAXIMUM level of depression experienced at any one point in the day.
5. Your AVERAGE level of pleasantness that day.
6. Your MAXIMUM level of pleasantness experienced that day.
7. Number of panic attacks experienced, if any.

Level of Anxiety/Depression/Pleasantness

0	1	2	3	4	5	6	7	8
None		Slight		Moderate		A lot		As much as I can imagine

Date	Average Anxiety	Maximum Anxiety	Average Depression	Maximum Depression	Average Pleasantness	Maximum Pleasantness	Panic Attacks

My Cycle of Panic and Anxiety

Name _____

Date _____ Time _____ Duration _____ (mins)

With: Family member _____ Friend _____ Stranger _____ Alone _____

Stressful situation: Yes/No   If yes, specify _____   Expected: Yes/No

Maximum Anxiety (Circle the number that applies)

0 ·········· 1 ·········· 2 ·········· 3 ·········· 4 ·········· 5 ·········· 6 ·········· 7 ·········· 8

None   Moderate   Extreme

Feelings in My Body

What I Do

What I Think

Session 4
Thinking Like a Detective

Chapter 5

Goals

- To learn to challenge your inaccurate thoughts by thinking like a detective

- To learn about the common myths and misconceptions about anxiety

Thinking Like a Detective

In this session, you will learn to challenge your errors in thinking by using skills similar to those that a detective might use. Just like a detective, you will need to examine the facts and situations around you in order to understand your anxiety-related thoughts.

The three steps to thinking like a detective are:

1. Treat your thoughts like guesses, not facts

2. Think about the evidence that supports your thought, and think about the evidence that goes against it

3. Come up with different ways of thinking about the situation

As you begin to focus on your thoughts, you may experience an increase in your anxiety. This is normal and to be expected. You may have been avoiding these sorts of thoughts for a long time now. Suddenly doing the opposite is bound to make you feel anxious. As you gain practice in thinking like a detective, your thoughts about panic will occur less frequently and will become easier to change.

How to Stop Overestimating

Think about a time when you predicted that something bad was going to happen and remember the thoughts you had. Ask yourself the following questions:

- How likely is it that my prediction will occur if I panic?

- How many times has that happened in the past when I panicked?

- What evidence do I have that it will happen? Is there any evidence that it will not happen?

- Have I ever seen or heard of that happening to anyone else?

- Are there any other possible reasons for these sensations?

Example

Situation: Going to school in the morning.

Anxious thoughts: *Once I get inside the classroom, I won't be able to breathe. I will be paralyzed with fear and won't be able to leave.*

We begin with the first thought.

Q: Would not being able to breathe be consistent with what I know about the purpose and activities of the fear system?

A: *Well, actually, the fear system increases breathing, to help prepare the body for action. So, I guess it doesn't make much sense to think that I wouldn't be able to breathe.*

Q: Is there any evidence that something is wrong with my body that would make me have trouble breathing during a panic attack?

A: *I guess not . . .*

Q: Does my past experience with panic attacks support my thought that I won't be able to breathe?

A: *Well, I've had lots of attacks in my life, but I don't always feel short of breath during an attack. If I only count the attacks when I did feel short of breath, I've probably had about 20. In those, I always felt like I couldn't breathe, but I didn't ever pass out or anything. I did breathe.*

Q: Then, what do I think the realistic chances are that I won't be able to breathe during a panic attack?

A: *Well, realistically, it is probably zero. It just feels higher.*

Q: What is the most likely thing that will happen?

A: *Based on previous times, I'll just feel short of breath and probably breathe really, really hard until the attack is over.*

Now let's look at the second thought, that you will somehow be trapped in the classroom.

Q: Would being "paralyzed with fear" and being trapped in the classroom as a result be consistent with what I know about how the fear system operates?

A: *Well, I don't really know. My legs feel weak and wobbly, but my fear system is actually designed to help me run or fight, and I guess it wouldn't make sense that the fear system wouldn't allow me to control the muscles in my body when I feel fear. So, I guess the changes aren't really consistent with being "paralyzed" or anything like that. Although, it sure does feel like that!*

Q: Does my past experience with panic attacks support my fear that I will be paralyzed and unable to escape the situation?

A: *Well, one time I had to run out of the classroom because I thought I'd die if I couldn't get out during a panic attack.*

Q: But were you able to easily exit the classroom?

A: *Yes, it wasn't a problem at all. It might have been a little embarrassing, because nobody knew where I was going. And, it just seemed like I was "paralyzed," I guess because it took a few seconds for me to get out of the room. My teacher came after me, and she was actually pretty understanding about what was happening. She just wanted me to tell her where I was going next time.*

Q: Then what is the real likelihood that you will actually be paralyzed with fear and unable to get out of the classroom?

A: *Well, it doesn't seem likely at all that I would be paralyzed. And, I guess if I wasn't paralyzed, then I could definitely get out of the room.*

Q: What is the most likely thing that will happen?

A: *If I ask my teacher if I can leave, I might have to wait a moment for her to respond and let me go, but I can always walk out of the classroom if I need to, because there really is no chance that I would be paralyzed by my panic and anxiety.*

How to Stop Thinking the Worst

You can use the detective strategy to challenge your catastrophic thinking as well. Remember, catastrophic thinking is when you think the worst is going to happen. When you start to think that the worst is going to happen, try asking yourself the following questions.

- What is the worst that can happen? How bad is that?

- So what if _____ happens?

- Could I cope? Have I been able to cope with _____ in the past?

- Even if _____ happens, can I live through it?

- Is _____ really so terrible?

Example

Situation: You are at the mall with your friends. All of a sudden, you feel shaky and notice that your heart is beating really, really fast—for seemingly no reason at all!

Anxious thoughts: *There is something wrong with my heart. Maybe I am having a heart attack! There is something really wrong with me!*

Your questions and answers might go something like this:

Q: Do I really have any clues to tell me something is really wrong with my heart that might explain what just happened in the mall?

A: *It just seemed to be going really fast for no reason at all! That doesn't seem normal.*

Q: No, but we did go to the pediatrician already, and he said that my heart was fine. But, could there still be something wrong with my heart?

A: *The doctor said all the tests I took showed that I had a healthy, normal heart. But, maybe he's wrong! There must be some test I haven't had yet!*

Q: OK, but, seriously—I don't think there are any big heart tests that the doctor forgot. So, are there any clues to tell me that something is wrong?

A: *No, it doesn't seem as though the doctor found any clues to suggest that something is wrong.*

Q: Do I have any reason to think he was a bad doctor?

A: *Probably not. When my mom took me to the emergency room a while ago because I thought I was having a heart problem, they didn't find anything wrong with my heart either.*

Q: Could the feelings I am experiencing actually be due to one of those "false alarms" in my nervous system, as though my sympathetic nervous system or breathing just suddenly got turned up a notch?

A: *Yeah, it might be that.*

Q: Were there any conditions that might have made that more likely?

A: *Well, I was around a bunch of people that I knew and feeling a little stressed about whether they would notice that I was feeling bad—but nothing bad actually happened.*

Q: Could the feelings possibly have been due to normal changes in my breathing, something I ate or drank, or a medication I took, or some other cause?

A: *Nothing I can think of really. I had a soda at lunch, but that's not too strange. I suppose that it could have been due to a change in my breathing, but I didn't really notice. Still, I guess I can't say for sure that it didn't change! I did climb a flight of stairs in the mall too.*

Q: So, I guess the possibilities are that I really do have a heart problem, a false alarm in my fear system, or some unnoticed change in my breathing. Let's think about the evidence for and against each of these possibilities.

A: *Well, in support of a heart problem, there is the fact that it was feeling as though it was beating very fast, although I'm learning that my sympathetic nervous system can actually make that happen too. Against the idea that I have a heart problem is the fact that I really have had these feelings many times before, and my doctor says that my tests are all normal. I don't have any real evidence of a heart problem. The idea of a false alarm in my nervous system seems like a good one because it would explain all the symptoms I was experiencing. Also, it seems as though these sorts of false alarms are really common with people who have panic disorder. Also, I was feeling stressed at the time and had had a cola earlier, which might have turned up my fear system. I can't think of any evidence against this idea. In support of a change in my breathing as the cause is the fact that increases in breathing can actually cause some of the feelings I had. Also, I had climbed a flight of stairs at the mall, which probably caused me to breathe harder for a while. Against that idea though is the fact that I wasn't aware of breathing any harder. Also, just climbing stairs doesn't usually cause me any problems. Or rather, my heart does probably beat faster when I climb stairs, but that's normal. This seemed different from that.*

Q: So, based on all these clues, which possibility seems the most likely?

A: *Considering all the possibilities and clues, I guess the false alarm explanation is much more likely than any of the other possibilities. Maybe my breathing had a little bit to do with it too.*

The Thinking Like a Detective form at the end of the chapter will help you challenge your anxious thoughts. Complete the form any time you find yourself overestimating or thinking the worst. You may photocopy the form from the book if necessary.

Myths and Misconceptions

Some common myths and misconceptions about anxiety include:

■ Going Crazy. Many people fear that they may go crazy or lose their minds when having a panic attack. Having panic sensations, however, is a normal reaction to danger signals. Rather than being crazy, it makes sense to have feelings of panic in response to something that is perceived as being scary.

Losing Control. Another common fear people have is that they will lose control during a panic attack and do something embarrassing or harmful. Panic attacks will not make you act without your knowledge. While you may be embarrassed, it usually won't be as bad as you think.

Nervous Collapse or Fainting. Some people think they might faint or lose consciousness during a panic attack. While this is not very common, even if it were to happen, it will not hurt you. At worst, it may be temporarily embarrassing.

Heart Attack. Heart pounding or racing is a common symptom of panic attacks. Some people mistake this sensation for a heart attack. Panic attacks cannot cause heart attacks and do not weaken your heart. Once the panic attack is over, your heart rate will return to normal.

The Panic Attack Will Never End. Sometimes it feels like the panic attack will keep on going forever. Eventually though, usually within a matter of minutes, the panic symptoms will start to fade on their own. The panic attack is just a temporary reaction to fear.

It is common for most teens and adults with panic disorder to believe that at least some of these myths may be true. But, more often, it is a lack of specific information about and fear of strong panic sensations that can lead you to make errors in your thinking about the causes and consequences of panic sensations. Try to use this new information when panic sensations arise to help combat any myths or misconceptions you may be holding about the consequences of panic attacks.

Homework

Review this chapter and complete the quiz

Continue recording the number of panic attacks and your daily levels of anxiety, depression, and pleasantness over the course of the next week using the Weekly Record found at the end of this chapter

Use the My Cycle of Panic and Anxiety form to record the details of each individual panic attack you experience

Use the Thinking Like a Detective form to challenge and disprove your panic-related thoughts. Try to add your thoughts to the form once a day, at a regular time and place. However, you may use the form more often if necessary.

Quiz

1. What are the three steps to thinking like a detective?

_____

_____

_____

2. What are some questions you can ask yourself to help you stop overestimating?

_____

_____

_____

_____

3. What are some questions you can ask yourself to help you stop thinking the worst?

_____

_____

_____

_____

4. What are some common myths and misconceptions about anxiety?

_____

_____

_____

_____

Thinking Like a Detective

Situation	Automatic Thought(s)	Emotions	Thinking Trap (Overestimating, Catastrophic Thinking)	Evidence For	Evidence Against	Alternative Thought

Weekly Record

Name: _____   Date: _____

Each evening, please make the following ratings, using the scale below:

1. Your AVERAGE level of anxiety of that day.
2. Your MAXIMUM level of anxiety experienced at any one point in the day.
3. Your AVERAGE level of depression that day.
4. Your MAXIMUM level of depression experienced at any one point in the day.
5. Your AVERAGE level of pleasantness that day.
6. Your MAXIMUM level of pleasantness experienced that day.
7. Number of panic attacks experienced, if any.

Level of Anxiety/Depression/Pleasantness

0	1	2	3	4	5	6	7	8
None		Slight		Moderate		A lot		As much as I can imagine

Date	Average Anxiety	Maximum Anxiety	Average Depression	Maximum Depression	Average Pleasantness	Maximum Pleasantness	Panic Attacks

My Cycle of Panic and Anxiety

Name _____

Date _____ Time _____ Duration _____ (mins)

With: Family member _____ Friend _____ Stranger _____ Alone _____

Stressful situation: Yes/No   If yes, specify _____   Expected: Yes/No

Maximum Anxiety (Circle the number that applies)

0 ········· 1 ········· 2 ········· 3 ········· 4 ········· 5 ········· 6 ········· 7 ········· 8

None   Moderate   Extreme

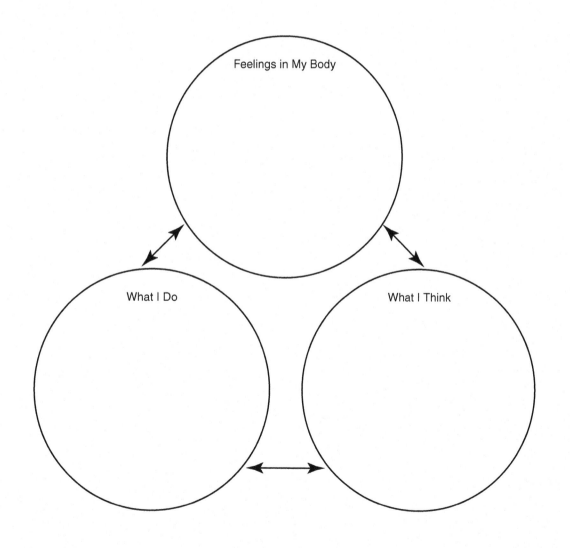

Session 5
Facing Scary Feelings

Goals

- To learn about conditioning and how it contributes to "out-of-the-blue" panic attacks

- To learn about exposure and how it can help you reduce feelings of anxiety and panic

- To try different exercises that will help you get used to scary feelings

Conditioning and Fear

When people have frightening experiences, they sometimes come to connect the fear with something that was present when the experience occurred. It might be some aspect of the place or situation where it happened, like the sound of a dentist's drill or a particular stretch of road. It might be an animal or object that was there at the time, like a dog or a needle. Or, it might be a physical sensation that occurred during the experience, like heart palpitations or a feeling of unreality. Often, these things are not dangerous in themselves but, because they were present during the frightening experience, any time the person is in that situation again, or comes upon that object, or notices that sensation, he may experience a sudden rush of fear. The process responsible for making this happen has a special name in psychology. It is called *conditioning*.

Conditioning is one way to explain unexpected panic attacks that seem to come from "out of the blue." Have you ever had the experience of becoming sick or vomiting after eating a particular food, and later felt sick at the mere mention or sight of the food? This is an example of conditioning; it is something you learn. Can you think of other examples? Are there things (such as a particular smell, or certain songs or music) that you have an automatic reaction to?

Because of conditioning, panic can occur in response to physical feelings that are very hard to recognize. Remember the hyperventilation exercise you did in Session 2? It showed you how even slight changes in your breathing can make you feel as if you are panicking. Then, because you are panicking for "no reason," you start to think panic thoughts such as, "I must be having a heart attack," or "I'm going crazy." One way to overcome conditioning is to break the connection between physical sensations and panic through exposure therapy.

Exposure Therapy

Exposure therapy is one of the most common ways of reducing excessive or inappropriate fear. It is extremely effective for helping people with panic disorder overcome their anxiety. In today's session, you will participate in specific exercises that will recreate the physical feelings of panic. You will "expose" yourself to panic sensations.

Because you may be avoiding certain situations that recreate the feelings and symptoms of panic, it is very important that you learn how to deal with these feelings. By experiencing scary feelings on a regular basis in a safe environment, you will begin to learn that the things you have been feeling during your panic attacks are not dangerous or harmful.

For this strategy to work, you will have to do the exercises over and over until your fear decreases and you get used to the feelings. This is called *habituation*. It is like riding a wave. Habituation will reduce feelings of panic over time, just like a wave naturally reduces in size as it reaches the beach. You need to "ride the wave" of panic until the fear comes down. Look at the curve shown in Figure 6.1. The dotted and dashed lines illustrate how repeated practice of exposures leads to a reduction in the intensity of panic feelings over time.

Exposing Yourself to Feared Sensations

Your therapist is going to conduct a variety of exercises that will cause you to feel anxiety symptoms most similar to those you feel when you have a panic attack. After your therapist demonstrates the exercise, you will do it on your own for as long as your therapist asks you to.

You will participate in the following exercises:

1. Shake your head from side to side (does not need to be done quickly) for 30 seconds

2. Place your head between your knees for 30 seconds, then quickly lift it to an upright position

Riding the "wave of anxiety"

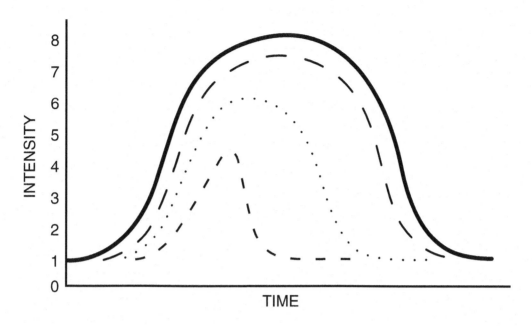

Figure 6.1 Habituation Curve

3. Run in place for 1 minute

4. Hold your breath for 30 seconds

5. Tense the muscles throughout your body for 1 minute or hold a push-up position for as long as possible

6. Spin in a chair (relatively quickly) for 1 minute

7. Hyperventilate for 1 minute

8. Breathe through a thin straw (such as a coffee stirrer or cocktail straw) for 2 minutes with nostrils held together

After each exercise, your therapist will ask you to describe the sensations you felt and to rate the strength of the sensations on a scale of 0–8 (0 meaning you did not experience any feelings of panic and 8 meaning that you felt the most intense feelings of panic possible). You will use the same scale to rate your level of anxiety during the exercise and the degree of similarity between the sensations you felt during the exercise and those you feel when you have an actual panic attack. Use these ratings to determine which of the exercises made you feel most like the way you feel when you have a panic attack. You will be asked to repeat these exercises as homework using the following instructions.

Exposure Instructions

1. On the Symptom Exposure Record found at the end of the chapter, write the exercise you are practicing (such as spinning in a chair) and the trial number (if you practice the exercise three times in a row, put "1" for the first time, "2" for the second time, and "3" for the third). Indicate whether you performed the exercise alone (Y) or with a parent or another person (N).

2. Do the exercise until you begin to feel physical sensations. Then continue the exercise for another 30 seconds (10 seconds for holding your breath or head shaking). Remember, your goal is to bring on those sensations so you can practice riding the wave of panic. If you experience only mild sensations after 30 seconds, try to continue the exercise until they reach moderate levels of intensity.

3. Focus on the physical feelings—don't distract yourself! Remember, the goal is to learn to be less afraid of these sensations by letting yourself experience them. Ride the wave!

4. After you stop the exercise, list any anxious thoughts you had, and practice "being a detective" by identifying and challenging them.

5. After you have decreased your anxiety to a mild level (2 or less), record your maximum anxiety experienced during the exercise (0–8). Also record your maximum intensity of physical sensations experienced during or after the exercise and rate the similarity of the sensations to those you experience during your naturally occurring panic attacks (0–8).

6. Repeat steps 1 through 5. Try to practice each exercise three times in a row each day. Your maximum anxiety level should start to go down with each practice as you learn to be less afraid of the physical feelings.

Homework

- Review this chapter and complete the quiz

- Continue recording the number of panic attacks and your daily levels of anxiety, depression, and pleasantness over the course of the next week using the Weekly Record found at the end of this chapter

- Use the My Cycle of Panic and Anxiety form to record the details of each individual panic attack you experience

- Choose three exercises from today's session that made you feel most like you were having an actual panic attack and repeat them at home. Record your results on the Symptom Exposure Record provided.

Quiz

1. What is conditioning?

_____

_____

_____

_____

2. How can you break the connection between physical sensations and panic?

_____

_____

_____

_____

3. What is habituation?

_____

_____

_____

_____

Symptom Exposure Record

For each symptom exposure exercise you engage in, describe what you did (such as spinning, or breathing through a straw) and the sensations you experienced during the exercise (dizzy, disoriented, short of breath). Then, just as you did in the session with your therapist, use a scale of 0–8 to rate the overall intensity of the sensations, how anxious or afraid you felt during the exercise, and the similarity of the sensations to those you typically feel during a panic attack. Finally, list any anxious thoughts you had during the exercise.

Exercise	Sensations	Intensity (0–8)	Anxiety/Fear (0–8)	Similarity (0–8)	Anxious Thoughts

Weekly Record

Name: _____   Date: _____

Each evening, please make the following ratings, using the scale below:

1. Your AVERAGE level of anxiety of that day.
2. Your MAXIMUM level of anxiety experienced at any one point in the day.
3. Your AVERAGE level of depression that day.
4. Your MAXIMUM level of depression experienced at any one point in the day.
5. Your AVERAGE level of pleasantness that day.
6. Your MAXIMUM level of pleasantness experienced that day.
7. Number of panic attacks experienced, if any.

Level of Anxiety/Depression/Pleasantness

0	1	2	3	4	5	6	7	8
None		Slight		Moderate		A lot		As much as I can imagine

Date	Average Anxiety	Maximum Anxiety	Average Depression	Maximum Depression	Average Pleasantness	Maximum Pleasantness	Panic Attacks

My Cycle of Panic and Anxiety

Name _____

Date _____ Time _____ Duration _____ (mins)

With: Family member _____ Friend _____ Stranger _____ Alone _____

Stressful situation: Yes/No   If yes, specify _____   Expected: Yes/No

Maximum Anxiety (Circle the number that applies)

0 ·········· 1 ·········· 2 ·········· 3 ·········· 4 ·········· 5 ·········· 6 ·········· 7 ·········· 8

None   Moderate   Extreme

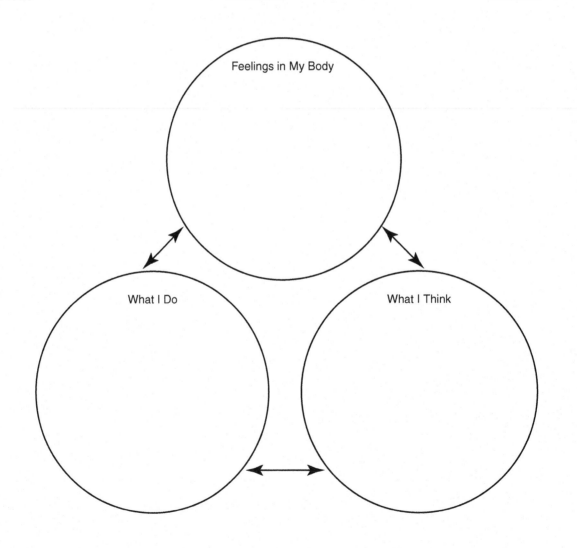

Sessions 6–10
Facing Feared Situations

Chapter 7

Goals

▪ To learn about avoidance and safety behaviors

▪ To begin exposing yourself to situations that make you feel anxious

Up until this point, you and your therapist have been focusing mostly on your thoughts and feelings related to panic and anxiety. During this final phase of the program, the focus will switch to your behaviors, specifically your avoidance and escape behaviors. Remember, a lot of people with panic disorder (PD) also suffer from something called *agoraphobia*. You learned about this in Chapter 1. Agoraphobia comes from the Latin words for "fear of the market place." It is defined as anxiety about being in places or situations that would be difficult to leave or where help might not be available if a panic attack were to occur.

Avoidance

We talked briefly about avoidance in Session 1 (see Chapter 2). Avoidance is any behavior used to reduce uncomfortable emotions or feelings. Avoidance can be obvious or hard to recognize (subtle). Examples of obvious avoidance are leaving a situation or place that makes you feel anxious or not engaging in certain activities because you are afraid that you will panic. Examples of subtle avoidance are carrying a good luck charm or distracting yourself. These kinds of subtle avoidance are called "safety behaviors," and we explain them in more detail later on in this chapter.

Think about the effect avoidance can have on a person's fear of a situation. Although avoidance may provide immediate relief, it only increases anxiety and fear in the long run. Think about summer vacation. For most students, it is hard to go back to school after summer vacation because they have been away from it for so long. They are used to hanging out with their friends, working part-time jobs, traveling with their family, and doing other things. They are not used to being in classes and doing homework. When they have to go back to school, it can be a little scary. This is similar to how avoidance works—by avoiding the situation, your fear only gets bigger. This is because when you avoid an anxiety-provoking situation or sensation, you never learn that the situation or sensation is not really dangerous, and you never develop confidence in your ability to handle it.

Although it feels good in the short term to avoid the source of your anxiety, in the long term it will make your PD worse. For example, you may avoid going to the movies with your friends because you are afraid you will have a panic attack, so avoiding the movies can give you a sense of relief at first. However, the longer you avoid going to the movies, the harder it becomes to get into the movie theater. This can lead to you avoiding not only the movies, but other similar activities like plays and concerts, until eventually you are avoiding all sorts of social activities such as going out to eat or attending parties. Your avoidance can "spread" to other situations. To stop this, you must begin confronting your feared situations on a regular basis until your anxiety comes down, just like you did last week when you exposed yourself to scary physical feelings.

Think of the last scary movie you saw. Imagine that you watched the movie over and over again, say 50 times. It is very likely that by the 50th time of seeing the movie, the things that made you jump or feel frightened would not seem as scary anymore. This is the concept of *habituation* you learned about last week (see Chapter 6). By repeatedly exposing yourself to the situations that scare you, you will get used to handling them, and they will no longer make you panic.

Safety Behaviors

Safety behaviors are things you do to make yourself feel safer or less anxious in a situation or to reduce uncomfortable sensations. Usually a logical connection is made between the safety behavior and some immediate objective. For example, some people may sit near an exit so that they can make a quick escape, while others may carry a good luck charm with them at all times. Examples of some common safety behaviors include:

- distracting yourself

- carrying or taking medication

- doing relaxation or slow breathing

- bringing someone with you when you go out

- bringing a water bottle, cell phone, or other item with you when you go somewhere

Although safety behaviors may make it possible for you to enter or stay in a situation rather than avoid or escape it altogether, they keep you from fully facing the situation. Also, the use of safety behaviors only keeps the anxiety alive and makes it worse in the long run, because you are not allowing yourself to fully experience the symptoms of anxiety.

It is very important that you do not use safety behaviors during your exposure exercises. You need to experience the situation and your anxiety fully, to learn that they are not so scary and that you can handle them.

Listing Safety Behaviors

Now that you have a full understanding of safety behaviors, work with your therapist to create a list of your own safety behaviors using the space provided.

My Safety Behaviors

1. _____

2. _____

3. _____

4. _____

5. _____

6. _____

7. _____

8. _____

9. _____

10. _____

Exposing Yourself to Feared Situations

Just as you exposed yourself to scary physical sensations last week, this week you will begin to expose yourself to scary situations. Your therapist will ask you to enter some of the situations that you normally avoid because you are afraid you will have a panic attack.

When you repeatedly face a feared situation, three important things happen:

1. Your thoughts about the dangerousness of the situation and your ability to cope with it change for the better. This reduces anxiety.

2. Conditioned fear reactions (see Chapter 6) to the situation are weakened and new, healthier associations are created.

3. You stop avoiding and feeling limited by fear. This interrupts the panic cycle.

Your therapist understands that it can be very scary for you to face the situations that you normally avoid and that doing so may even cause panic attacks. However, for exposure therapy to be effective, you must experience those emotions and the physical feelings that go along with them. Unless you learn that you can survive the anxiety, you may continue to feel afraid and avoid the things that scare you. The stronger your anxiety during exposure, the more confident you will become of your ability to cope with the fear.

Your Fear and Avoidance Hierarchy

Together with your therapist, you will create a list of 10 situations that you tend to avoid because you are afraid that you will have a panic attack. Use the Fear and Avoidance Hierarchy (FAH) form provided and rank your level of fear for each situation on a scale of 0–8, with 0 meaning you do not fear the situation at all and 8 meaning that you very much fear the situation. Also rate your level of avoidance using the same scale, with 0 meaning you never avoid the situation and 8 meaning you always avoid it. Examples of situations include going to the movies, eating out in a restaurant, going to a party or dance, and other similar activities. After creating your hierarchy, you and your therapist will choose one situation for you to practice facing today. Over the course of the next few weeks, you will continue to practice facing the feared situations on your FAH, working your way up to those that cause you the most anxiety.

Fear and Avoidance Hierarchy

Name _____   Date_____

0·········1·········2·········3·········4·········5·········6·········7·········8

| no fear | a little fear | moderate fear | a lot of fear | very much fear |
| never avoid | rarely avoid | sometimes avoid | often avoid | always avoid |

	Description	Fear 0-8	Avoid 0-8	Did you do? Y/N
1. The worst situation				
2. The second worst situation				
3. The third worst situation				
4. The fourth worst situation				
5. The fifth worst situation				
6. The sixth worst situation				
7. The seventh worst situation				
8. The eighth worst situation				
9. The ninth worst situation				
10. The tenth worst situation				

This next phase of the program is crucial to your success. Your homework for the remaining weeks of treatment is to practice exposures, keeping the following guidelines in mind.

Exposure Guidelines

1. During your exposure practices, let the anxiety wash over you without resistance. It will not harm you. Allow yourself to feel the sensations that occur, notice the thoughts they evoke, and observe your behavior.

2. If you experience a panic attack during the course of an exercise, try to stay in the situation and ride out the wave of panic. Exposure exercises are not designed to cause panic attacks, but they do occur occasionally. This is helpful, because they allow you to test your overestimating and catastrophic thoughts (see Chapter 4) and gain confidence in your ability to survive even the worst-case scenario.

3. If you stop an exposure before it is over, try it again. Review what happened and challenge your thoughts. It is unlikely that the thing you most feared would happen actually did. Become a detective (see Chapter 5) and review the evidence to support your thoughts, as well as the evidence that goes against them. Generate alternative thoughts that are more accurate. After doing this, give yourself a few minutes to regain composure and then attempt the exposure again.

4. Collect mementos or souvenirs of your accomplishments (things like movie ticket stubs, postcards, photographs) to show your therapist that you were able to handle situations that normally scare you.

5. The goal of exposure therapy is to maximize anxiety. This is essential for exposure to work. If you find that you are having fun during your practices, the exposures are too easy and need to be made more difficult. There will be time to enjoy yourself after treatment ends. However, you may feel free to reward yourself for successful exposures.

6. Remember, it is very important that you do *not* engage in any safety behaviors as you practice your exposure exercises.

As you complete your exposure assignments, be sure to record them on the Situational Exposure Record provided at the end of the chapter. Additional copies of the form can be found in the appendix at the back of the book. Alternatively, you may make photocopies.

Homework

- Review this chapter and complete the quiz

- Continue recording the number of panic attacks and your daily levels of anxiety, depression, and pleasantness over the course of the next week using the Weekly Record found at the end of this chapter

- Use the My Cycle of Panic and Anxiety form to record the details of each individual panic attack you experience

- Repeat the in-session exposure at home and record it on the Situational Exposure Record

- Put yourself in situations from your FAH as planned and record them on the Situational Exposure Record

- Review exposure instructions as needed

Quiz

1. How does avoidance make panic disorder worse?

_____

_____

_____

_____

_____

2. What are safety behaviors?

_____

_____

_____

_____

_____

3. Why is it important to feel anxious during exposure?

_____

_____

_____

_____

_____

Situational Exposure Record

Date and time: _____

Exposure task: _____

Prior to the task:

Anticipatory anxiety (o–8): _____

Automatic thoughts about the task:

_____

_____

_____

Reevaluate your automatic thoughts about the task:

_____

_____

_____

After completing the task:

Number of minutes you did the task: _____

Maximum anxiety experienced during the task (o–8): _____

Anxiety at the end of the task (o–8): _____

Any attempts to avoid your emotions (distraction, safety signals, etc.)?

_____

_____

_____

Additional comments:

_____

_____

_____

_____

Weekly Record

Name: _____   Date: _____

Each evening, please make the following ratings, using the scale below:

1. Your AVERAGE level of anxiety of that day.
2. Your MAXIMUM level of anxiety experienced at any one point in the day.
3. Your AVERAGE level of depression that day.
4. Your MAXIMUM level of depression experienced at any one point in the day.
5. Your AVERAGE level of pleasantness that day.
6. Your MAXIMUM level of pleasantness experienced that day.
7. Number of panic attacks experienced, if any.

Level of Anxiety/Depression/Pleasantness

0	1	2	3	4	5	6	7	8
None		Slight		Moderate		A lot		As much as I can imagine

Date	Average Anxiety	Maximum Anxiety	Average Depression	Maximum Depression	Average Pleasantness	Maximum Pleasantness	Panic Attacks

My Cycle of Panic and Anxiety

Name _____

Date _____ Time _____ Duration _____ (mins)

With: Family member _____ Friend _____ Stranger _____ Alone _____

Stressful situation: Yes/No   If yes, specify _____   Expected: Yes/No

Maximum Anxiety (Circle the number that applies)

0 ·············· 1 ·············· 2 ·············· 3 ·············· 4 ·············· 5 ·············· 6 ·············· 7 ·············· 8

None   Moderate   Extreme

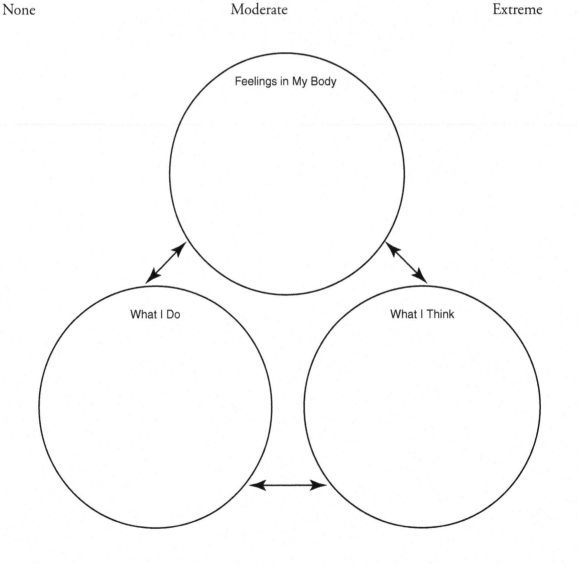

Session 11
The End of Treatment

Chapter 8

Goals

- To evaluate your progress

- To develop a plan for practicing skills on your own after treatment has ended

- To celebrate!

How Did You Do?

Now that you are nearing the end of treatment, it is important to look back at everything you have learned and evaluate your progress. Take a look at the Fear and Avoidance Hierarchy you created in Session 6. Review the situations listed and re-rate your level of fear and avoidance for each one using a new form. You should see a noticeable improvement (your ratings should have gone down).

Also review the My Goals form you completed in the first session. Identify which goals have been achieved and which ones still need more work.

Use the Taking Stock of All You've Accomplished form to write down your feelings about therapy. The answers you give to the questions will show you just how well you have done in this program.

Fear and Avoidance Hierarchy

Name _____   Date_____

0········1·········2·········3·········4·········5·········6·········7·········8

| no fear | a little fear | moderate fear | a lot of fear | very much fear |
| never avoid | rarely avoid | sometimes avoid | often avoid | always avoid |

	Description	Fear 0-8	Avoid 0-8	Did you do? Y/N
1. The worst situation				
2. The second worst situation				
3. The third worst situation				
4. The fourth worst situation				
5. The fifth worst situation				
6. The sixth worst situation				
7. The seventh worst situation				
8. The eighth worst situation				
9. The ninth worst situation				
10. The tenth worst situation				

Taking Stock of All You've Accomplished

1. What do you remember about the first time you came to treatment?

_____

_____

2. What was one of the most memorable experiences from therapy?

_____

_____

3. What was the most important thing you learned from therapy?

_____

_____

4. What will you never forget?

_____

_____

5. What anxieties have you overcome or reduced significantly?

_____

_____

6. What coping thoughts are most meaningful to you?

_____

_____

_____

7. What would you tell other people your age who are having a hard time?

_____

_____

_____

8. What is different about you now, compared to when you first began meeting with your therapist?

_____

_____

_____

9. Do you see differences in how you react to stressful events? What are they?

_____

_____

_____

10. What do you hope for the future?

_____

_____

_____

Developing a Practice Plan

Work together with your therapist to develop a list of assignments to do during the next month, focusing on areas where you are still experiencing problems. Write out your plan on the Becoming Your Own Therapist form provided here. Be sure to include as much detail about each individual assignment as possible. You should also schedule specific time for practicing tasks. Just as it helps to schedule specific times to go to the gym or health club if one is working on a fitness program, it is important to schedule specific times to exercise panic skills. Practicing skills repeatedly in real-life situations is the most important and essential part of treatment. The more often you practice, the better.

Becoming Your Own Therapist

1. What anxieties or other difficulties remain?

_____

_____

_____

2. What specific situations do you need to confront (through exposure or other practices) to overcome the remaining difficulties?

_____

_____

_____

3. What specific goals do you need to set for yourself to continue to improve in these areas and meet your hopes for the future?

_____

_____

_____

4. What are the specific automatic thoughts that continue to make you anxious as you think about these goals and situations? What evidence do you have to challenge these thoughts?

_____

_____

_____

5. What specific things are you going to practice over the next 4 weeks in order to maintain your progress and keep working toward your goals (such as exposures, coping thoughts, etc.)?

_____

_____

_____

Preparing for the Future

It is normal to feel some fear about ending treatment. You may be worried about your ability to keep improving in the months ahead without the help of your therapist. Think about your expectations for the end of treatment and ask yourself the following questions:

- How do you think things will go in the next several months?

- How confident are you that you will be able to maintain or extend your improvement?

- Do you anticipate any difficulties?

Discuss your thoughts with your therapist.

Normal Anxiety, Lapse, and Relapse

Anxiety and panic symptoms typically fluctuate over time. This is the normal course of events. Symptoms are likely to increase during periods of stress. Troubles at school or at home, and conflicts with friends or significant others can contribute to anxiety and panic attacks. Even positive events like moving to a new home or going on vacation can cause stress, which can increase feelings of anxiety and panic. If you are sick, you may experience an increase in anxiety as well. Some illnesses cause symptoms similar to those caused by anxiety. If you have a cold, your chest may feel tight and congested, and you may have trouble breathing. If you have the flu, you may feel weak and experience hot flushes. In addition, some medications like decongestants can have stimulating effects that may cause panic-like sensations.

It is important to know the difference between normal anxiety, a lapse or setback, and a full-blown relapse.

Normal Anxiety

Everyone feels anxious sometimes, and about 30% of the population experience occasional panic attacks. People who have had panic disorder clearly are in that 30%. The experience of anxiety during stressful periods, and even occasional panic attacks, are normal. They should not worry you. It is important that you don't misinterpret or overreact to normal anxiety.

Lapse or Setback

A "lapse" is a slip or partial loss of improvement. Lapses are different from normal anxiety in that lapses are more intense and last longer. If you experience a panic attack, it does not mean you have experienced a lapse, especially if you were able to handle it. If you experience a small increase in your agoraphobia or avoidance, and it grows over time, this would be a lapse.

Lapses may be due to stressful situations or personal problems or may simply be due to lack of practice of anxiety management skills. It is hard to stick to a diet or exercise program, especially when things are going well. Just as pounds can creep back on when a person cheats on a diet, symptoms can reemerge if you don't practice the skills you have learned in this program. If you experience a lapse, take it as a sign that you need more practice. Continued practice of your skills can prevent a lapse from turning into a relapse.

Relapse

A "relapse" is a full and persistent return of symptoms or avoidance to pretreatment levels or higher. Relapses typically begin as lapses that are not addressed. They can be prevented if you apply effective coping strategies in high-risk situations and when lapses occur.

Symptom fluctuations and even occasional lapses are common and should be anticipated. If you take every occurrence of anxiety in your life to mean that you are relapsing, you will become discouraged and may even think that treatment did not help. It is important to keep things in perspective. If you find yourself thinking negative thoughts about your normal anxiety, use the skills you learned (become a detective) to challenge them and change the way you're thinking.

Plan Ahead

Because your symptoms are likely to increase from time to time, it is important to anticipate that and have a plan for how to respond. The earlier and more aggressive the response, the more likely the increases can be nipped in the bud.

Use the Planning Ahead form provided to record situations or stressful events that might occur in the next several months (or longer) that could possibly cause an increase or lapse in panic symptoms. Write down what anxious thoughts might return, what sensations might again begin to scare you, and what avoidance or safety behaviors might creep back. Then identify the strategies you could use to address each of these slips. Remember not to include safety behaviors such as cutting down on caffeine, taking medication, seeking or giving yourself simple reassurance, and avoiding stressful situations. These may provide short-term relief, but will only increase your anxiety in the long run.

It helps to *rehearse* using your strategies before you have a lapse. To do this, imagine as vividly as possible a real-life situation in which you may experience a lapse of the predicted thoughts, symptoms, and behaviors. Then imagine yourself carrying out the planned interventions and regaining control. Do rehearsals frequently during the next month so that you will be ready for lapses when they happen.

Planning Ahead

SITUATION	ANTICIPATED THOUGHTS	ANTICIPATED FEELINGS	ANTICIPATED BEHAVIORS
School field trip	I will panic on the bus and faint	Dizzy, sweaty, lightheaded	I'll pretend to be sick that day so I don't have to go
	STRATEGY	STRATEGY	STRATEGY
	Think like a detective and generate alternative thoughts	Perform symptom exposure to remind myself that the feelings aren't dangerous	Imagine being in the situation and handling my panic if it occurs
SITUATION	ANTICIPATED THOUGHTS	ANTICIPATED FEELINGS	ANTICIPATED BEHAVIORS
	STRATEGY	STRATEGY	STRATEGY
SITUATION	ANTICIPATED THOUGHTS	ANTICIPATED FEELINGS	ANTICIPATED BEHAVIORS
	STRATEGY	STRATEGY	STRATEGY

Congratulations!

Congratulations on completing the treatment! You should be very proud of all you have accomplished in these last 12 weeks. You learned a lot about the nature of anxiety and panic attacks, and the ways that thoughts, feelings, and behaviors work together to bring on the physical feelings that we call "panic." Most importantly, you have learned that these physical feelings are not harmful, and that if you are not afraid of them, surprisingly, they start to go away. You are now able to "ride the wave" of your panic.

You have worked hard in treatment, and it is very important to praise yourself for a job well done. Your family is undoubtedly proud of you, and you should be proud of yourself! You might think of a special reward you can give to yourself, like asking your parents to make your favorite dinner, going on a trip to the mall, or getting together with friends to do an activity you enjoy. One of the greatest rewards for feeling better is that you now have the ability to do the things you love to do! So go enjoy something fun, as a reward to yourself. And give yourself a pat on the back.

Final Quiz

1. What is the difference between normal anxiety, a lapse, and a relapse?

_____

_____

_____

_____

_____

2. What are the three kinds of slips that you should watch out for?

_____

_____

_____

_____

_____

3. What can you do to prepare for lapses?

_____

_____

_____

_____

_____

A Forms

My Cycle of Panic and Anxiety

Name _____

Date _____ Time _____ Duration _____ (mins)

With: Family member _____ Friend _____ Stranger _____ Alone _____

Stressful situation: Yes/No   If yes, specify _____   Expected: Yes/No

Maximum Anxiety (Circle the number that applies)

0 ·········· 1 ·········· 2 ·········· 3 ·········· 4 ·········· 5 ·········· 6 ·········· 7 ·········· 8

None   Moderate   Extreme

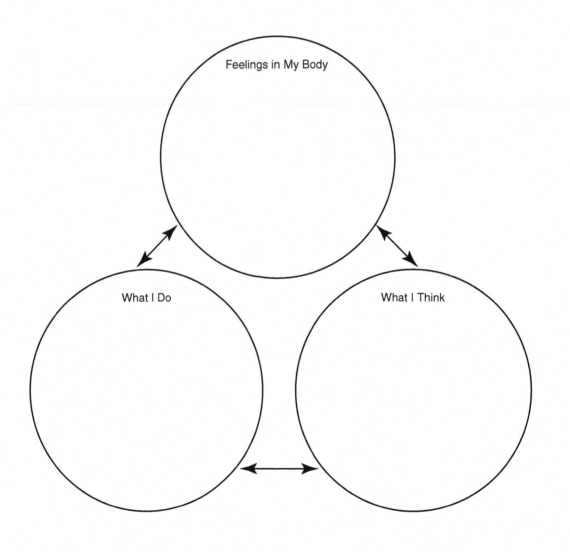

My Cycle of Panic and Anxiety

Name _____

Date _____ Time _____ Duration _____ (mins)

With: Family member _____ Friend _____ Stranger _____ Alone _____

Stressful situation: Yes/No   If yes, specify _____   Expected: Yes/No

Maximum Anxiety (Circle the number that applies)

0 ·········· 1 ·········· 2 ·········· 3 ·········· 4 ·········· 5 ·········· 6 ·········· 7 ·········· 8

None   Moderate   Extreme

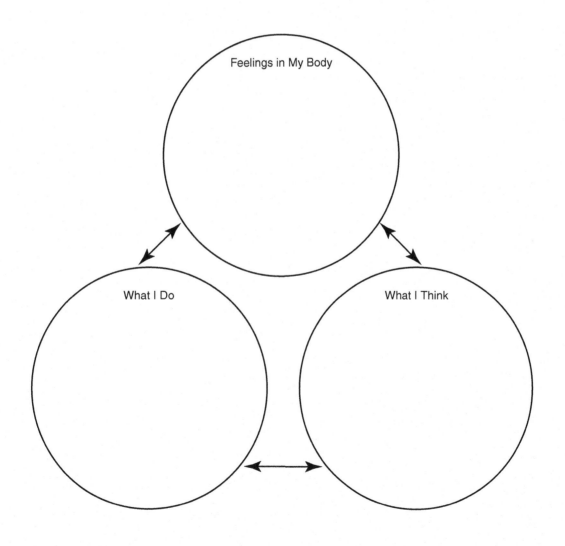

My Cycle of Panic and Anxiety

Name _____

Date _____ Time _____ Duration _____ (mins)

With: Family member _____ Friend _____ Stranger _____ Alone _____

Stressful situation: Yes/No   If yes, specify _____   Expected: Yes/No

Maximum Anxiety (Circle the number that applies)

0 ·············· I ·············· 2 ·············· 3 ·············· 4 ·············· 5 ·············· 6 ·············· 7 ·············· 8

None   Moderate   Extreme

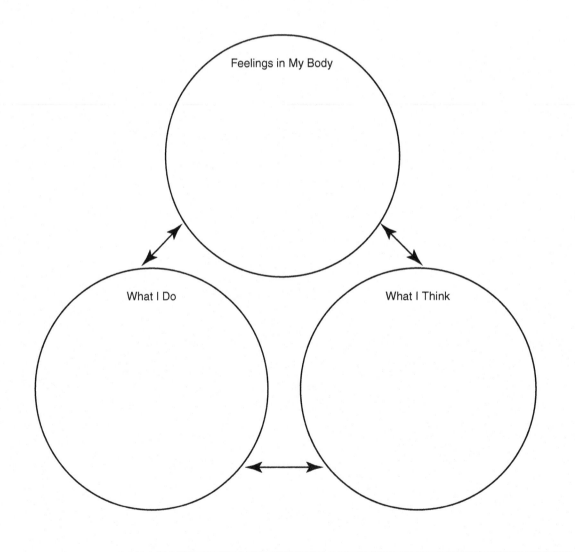

My Cycle of Panic and Anxiety

Name _____

Date _____ Time _____ Duration _____ (mins)

With: Family member _____ Friend _____ Stranger _____ Alone _____

Stressful situation: Yes/No   If yes, specify _____   Expected: Yes/No

Maximum Anxiety (Circle the number that applies)

0 ·········· 1 ·········· 2 ·········· 3 ·········· 4 ·········· 5 ·········· 6 ·········· 7 ·········· 8

None   Moderate   Extreme

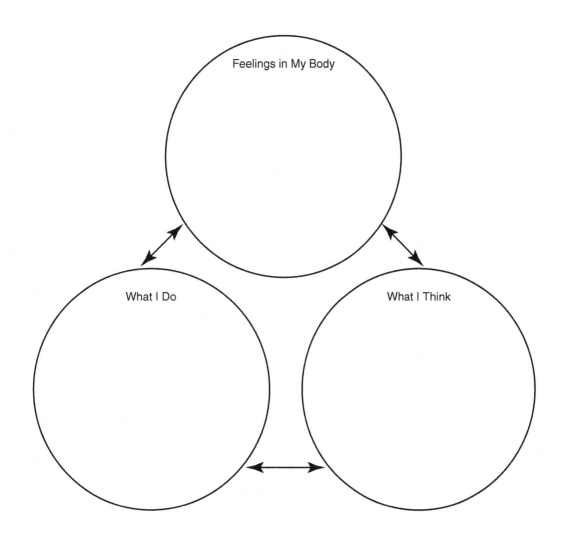

My Cycle of Panic and Anxiety

Name _____

Date _____ Time _____ Duration _____ (mins)

With: Family member _____ Friend _____ Stranger _____ Alone _____

Stressful situation: Yes/No   If yes, specify _____   Expected: Yes/No

Maximum Anxiety (Circle the number that applies)

0 ·········· 1 ·········· 2 ·········· 3 ·········· 4 ·········· 5 ·········· 6 ·········· 7 ·········· 8

None   Moderate   Extreme

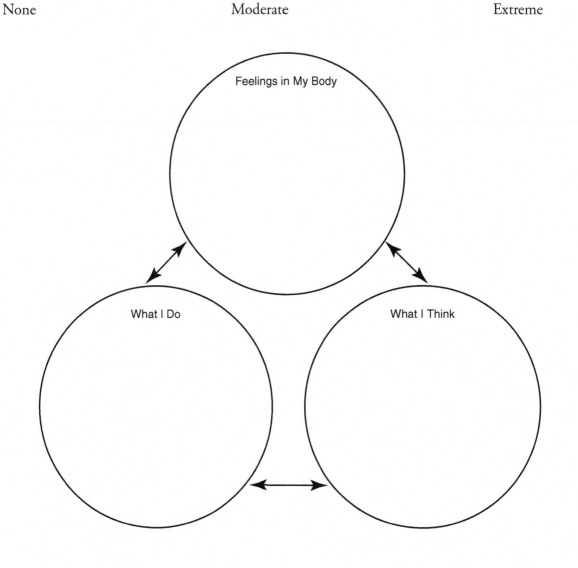

Weekly Record

Name: _____   Date: _____

Each evening, please make the following ratings, using the scale below:

1. Your AVERAGE level of anxiety of that day.
2. Your MAXIMUM level of anxiety experienced at any one point in the day.
3. Your AVERAGE level of depression that day.
4. Your MAXIMUM level of depression experienced at any one point in the day.
5. Your AVERAGE level of pleasantness that day.
6. Your MAXIMUM level of pleasantness experienced that day.
7. Number of panic attacks experienced, if any.

Level of Anxiety/Depression/Pleasantness

0	1	2	3	4	5	6	7	8
None		Slight		Moderate		A lot		As much as I can imagine

Date	Average Anxiety	Maximum Anxiety	Average Depression	Maximum Depression	Average Pleasantness	Maximum Pleasantness	Panic Attacks

Weekly Record

Name: _____   Date: _____

Each evening, please make the following ratings, using the scale below:

1. Your AVERAGE level of anxiety of that day.
2. Your MAXIMUM level of anxiety experienced at any one point in the day.
3. Your AVERAGE level of depression that day.
4. Your MAXIMUM level of depression experienced at any one point in the day.
5. Your AVERAGE level of pleasantness that day.
6. Your MAXIMUM level of pleasantness experienced that day.
7. Number of panic attacks experienced, if any.

Level of Anxiety/Depression/Pleasantness

0	1	2	3	4	5	6	7	8
None		Slight		Moderate		A lot		As much as I can imagine

Date	Average Anxiety	Maximum Anxiety	Average Depression	Maximum Depression	Average Pleasantness	Maximum Pleasantness	Panic Attacks

Weekly Record

Name: _____   Date: _____

Each evening, please make the following ratings, using the scale below:

1. Your AVERAGE level of anxiety of that day.
2. Your MAXIMUM level of anxiety experienced at any one point in the day.
3. Your AVERAGE level of depression that day.
4. Your MAXIMUM level of depression experienced at any one point in the day.
5. Your AVERAGE level of pleasantness that day.
6. Your MAXIMUM level of pleasantness experienced that day.
7. Number of panic attacks experienced, if any.

Level of Anxiety/Depression/Pleasantness

0	1	2	3	4	5	6	7	8
None		Slight		Moderate		A lot		As much as I can imagine

Date	Average Anxiety	Maximum Anxiety	Average Depression	Maximum Depression	Average Pleasantness	Maximum Pleasantness	Panic Attacks

Weekly Record

Name: _____ Date: _____

Each evening, please make the following ratings, using the scale below:

1. Your AVERAGE level of anxiety of that day.
2. Your MAXIMUM level of anxiety experienced at any one point in the day.
3. Your AVERAGE level of depression that day.
4. Your MAXIMUM level of depression experienced at any one point in the day.
5. Your AVERAGE level of pleasantness that day.
6. Your MAXIMUM level of pleasantness experienced that day.
7. Number of panic attacks experienced, if any.

Level of Anxiety/Depression/Pleasantness

0	1	2	3	4	5	6	7	8
None		Slight		Moderate		A lot		As much as I can imagine

Date	Average Anxiety	Maximum Anxiety	Average Depression	Maximum Depression	Average Pleasantness	Maximum Pleasantness	Panic Attacks

Weekly Record

Name: _____ Date: _____

Each evening, please make the following ratings, using the scale below:

1. Your AVERAGE level of anxiety of that day.
2. Your MAXIMUM level of anxiety experienced at any one point in the day.
3. Your AVERAGE level of depression that day.
4. Your MAXIMUM level of depression experienced at any one point in the day.
5. Your AVERAGE level of pleasantness that day.
6. Your MAXIMUM level of pleasantness experienced that day.
7. Number of panic attacks experienced, if any.

Level of Anxiety/Depression/Pleasantness

0	1	2	3	4	5	6	7	8
None		Slight		Moderate		A lot		As much as I can imagine

Date	Average Anxiety	Maximum Anxiety	Average Depression	Maximum Depression	Average Pleasantness	Maximum Pleasantness	Panic Attacks

Situational Exposure Record

Date and time: _____

Exposure task: _____

Prior to the task:

Anticipatory anxiety (0–8): _____

Automatic thoughts about the task:

_____

_____

_____

Reevaluate your automatic thoughts about the task:

_____

_____

_____

After completing the task:

Number of minutes you did the task: _____

Maximum anxiety experienced during the task (0–8): _____

Anxiety at the end of the task (0–8): _____

Any attempts to avoid your emotions (distraction, safety signals, etc.)?

_____

_____

_____

Additional comments:

_____

_____

Situational Exposure Record

Date and time: _____

Exposure task: _____

Prior to the task:

Anticipatory anxiety (0–8): _____

Automatic thoughts about the task:

_____

_____

_____

Reevaluate your automatic thoughts about the task:

_____

_____

_____

After completing the task:

Number of minutes you did the task: _____

Maximum anxiety experienced during the task (0–8): _____

Anxiety at the end of the task (0–8): _____

Any attempts to avoid your emotions (distraction, safety signals, etc.)?

_____

_____

_____

Additional comments:

_____

_____

_____

Situational Exposure Record

Date and time: _____

Exposure task: _____

Prior to the task:

Anticipatory anxiety (0–8): _____

Automatic thoughts about the task:

_____

_____

_____

Reevaluate your automatic thoughts about the task:

_____

_____

_____

After completing the task:

Number of minutes you did the task: _____

Maximum anxiety experienced during the task (0–8): _____

Anxiety at the end of the task (0–8): _____

Any attempts to avoid your emotions (distraction, safety signals, etc.)?

_____

_____

_____

Additional comments:

_____

_____

_____

Situational Exposure Record

Date and time: _____

Exposure task: _____

Prior to the task:

Anticipatory anxiety (0–8): _____

Automatic thoughts about the task:

_____

_____

_____

Reevaluate your automatic thoughts about the task:

_____

_____

_____

After completing the task:

Number of minutes you did the task: _____

Maximum anxiety experienced during the task (0–8): _____

Anxiety at the end of the task (0–8): _____

Any attempts to avoid your emotions (distraction, safety signals, etc.)?

_____

_____

_____

Additional comments:

_____

_____

_____

Situational Exposure Record

Date and time: _____

Exposure task: _____

Prior to the task:

Anticipatory anxiety (0–8): _____

Automatic thoughts about the task:

_____

_____

_____

Reevaluate your automatic thoughts about the task:

_____

_____

_____

After completing the task:

Number of minutes you did the task: _____

Maximum anxiety experienced during the task (0–8): _____

Anxiety at the end of the task (0–8): _____

Any attempts to avoid your emotions (distraction, safety signals, etc.)?

_____

_____

_____

Additional comments:

_____

_____

_____

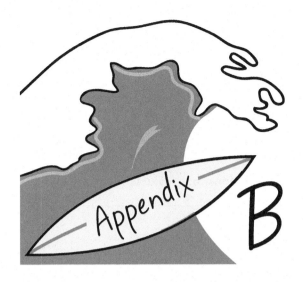

Appendix B

Quiz Answers

Chapter 1

1. What are some of the symptoms of a panic attack?

   Answer: Heart pounding or rapid heartbeat; sweating; trembling or shaking; shortness of breath or smothering sensations; feeling of choking; chest pain or discomfort; nausea or stomach discomfort; feeling dizzy, unsteady, lightheaded, or faint; feeling that the surroundings are unreal or of being detached from oneself; numbness or tingling sensations; chills or hot flashes; fear of losing control or going crazy; fear of dying.

2. What is "agoraphobia"?

   Answer: A pattern of avoiding certain places or situations (often where a person fears a panic attack may occur or situations where help may not be available).

3. What are the two necessary features of Panic Disorder?

   Answer: 1) Having at least two panic attacks that seem to come from "out of the blue." 2) The effects of the attacks – including worry about having more attacks or the attacks causing harm – significantly affect the person's life for at least a month.

Chapter 2

1. What are triggers? Give examples of internal and external triggers.

   Answer: Triggers are causes of panic. Internal triggers include negative thoughts and physical sensations. External triggers are particular situations that make you feel anxious like having to give an oral presentation in class.

2. What does the "fight-or-flight response" prepare your body to do?

   Answer: To either confront the threat and deal with it (fight), or get as far away from the threat as quickly as possible (flight).

3. What are the three parts of anxiety? Give examples of each.

   Answer: Feelings: fast heartbeat, dizziness, feeling unreal, sweating, etc.
   Thoughts: "I'm losing control," "I'm dying," etc.
   Behaviors: holding your breath, pacing, distracting yourself, avoiding, etc.

Chapter 3

1. What are some of the physical sensations of the fight-or-flight response?

   Answer: Heart beating fast, cold hands, chest tightness, breathlessness, sweating, blurred vision or spots in front of the eyes, dry mouth, muscle tension/aches, trembling.

2. What is hyperventilation?

   Answer: Hyperventilation is when you breathe faster and deeper than is necessary.

3. What was the purpose of the hyperventilation exercise?

   Answer: To demonstrate that simply overbreathing can cause symptoms similar to those experienced during panic.

Chapter 4

1. What are panic thoughts?

    Answer: Thoughts about how your anxiety is affecting you, like you are dying or losing control.

2. What are the two types of anxious thoughts that people with Panic Disorder commonly have?

    Answer: Overestimating thoughts and catastrophic thoughts (thinking the worst).

3. What is overestimating?

    Answer: Thinking the odds that something bad is going to happen are higher than they really are.

4. What is catastrophic thinking?

    Answer: Thinking that the worst thing imaginable is going to happen.

Chapter 5

1. What are the three steps to thinking like a detective?

    Answer: 1. Treat your thoughts like guesses, not facts; 2. Think about the evidence that supports your thought and think about the evidence that goes against it; 3. Come up with different ways of thinking about the situation.

2. What are some questions you can ask yourself to help you stop overestimating?

    Answer: How likely is it that my prediction will occur if I panic? How many times has that happened in the past when I panicked? What evidence do I have that it will happen? Is there any evidence that it will not happen? Have I ever seen or heard of that happening to anyone else? Are there any other possible reasons for these sensations?

3. What are some questions you can ask yourself to help you stop thinking the worst?

Answer: What is the worst that can happen? How bad is that? So what if _____ happens? Could I cope? Have I been able to cope with _____ in the past? Even if _____ happens, can I live through it? Is _____ really so terrible?

4. What are some common myths and misconceptions about anxiety?

    Answer: Going Crazy, Losing Control, Nervous Collapse or Fainting, Heart Attack, The Panic Attack Will Never End.

Chapter 6

1. What is conditioning?

    Answer: Coming to connect a feeling with something that was present when it occurred.

2. How can you break the connection between physical sensations and panic?

    Answer: Exposure therapy. By experiencing scary feelings on a regular basis in a safe environment, you learn that the things you have been feeling during your panic attacks are not dangerous or harmful.

3. What is habituation?

    Answer: Getting used to feelings through repeated exposure. It is like riding a wave of panic until the fear comes down.

Chapter 7

1. How does avoidance make panic disorder worse?

    Answer: It makes your fear get bigger. The fear can also spread to other situations.

2. What are safety behaviors?

    Answer: Things you do to make yourself feel safer or less anxious in a situation or to reduce uncomfortable sensations.

3. Why is it important to feel anxious during exposure?

Answer: You have to learn that you can survive the anxiety in order to overcome your fear and feel confident in your ability to cope.

Chapter 8

1. What is the difference between normal anxiety, a lapse, and a relapse?

Answer: It is normal to experience increases in anxiety (even panic attacks) during stressful periods. A "lapse" is a more intense and longer period of anxiety with growing avoidance. A "relapse" is a full and persistent return of symptoms or avoidance to pretreatment levels or higher.

2. What are the three kinds of slips that you should watch out for?

Answer: 1) anxious thoughts 2) scary physical sensations 3) avoidance or safety behaviors

3. What can you do to prepare for lapses?

Answer: Keep practicing the skills learned in therapy. Have a plan for how to respond to lapses. Rehearse by imagining situations and your strategies for handling them ahead of time.

CPSIA information can be obtained at www.ICGtesting.com
Printed in the USA
BVOW10s2135031115

425525BV00008B/13/P